Tales From The Wheelhouse
Adventures Aboard the Denali

by
Gary Gorss

Fair winds and following seas

Gary (captain Ace)

TRAFFORD

Edited by Linda Suarez

Cover illustration by Jennifer Taylor

Printed in Victoria, Canada

**National Library of Canada
Cataloguing in Publication Data**

Gorss, Gary, 1956-
  Tales from the wheelhouse : adventures aboard the Denali/
Gary Gorss ; editor, Linda Suarez.
ISBN 1-55395-061-5
  1. American wit and humor. I. Suarez, Linda II. Title.
PN6231.S15G67 2002   813'.6   C2002-904631-9

TRAFFORD

This book was published *on-demand* in cooperation with Trafford Publishing. On-demand publishing is a unique process and service of making a book available for retailsale to the public taking advantage of on-demand manufacturing and Internet marketing. **On-demand publishing** includes promotions, retail sales, manufacturing, order fulfilment, accounting and collecting royalties on behalf of the author.

Suite 6E, 2333 Government St., Victoria, B.C. V8T 4P4, CANADA
Phone   250-383-6864   Toll-free   1-888-232-4444 (Canada & US)
Fax   250-383-6804   E-mail   sales@trafford.com
Web site   www.trafford.com
TRAFFORD PUBLISHING IS A DIVISION OF TRAFFORD HOLDINGS LTD.
Trafford Catalogue #02-0773   www.trafford.com/robots/02-0773.html

10   9   8   7   6   5

Dedicated to my wife
Serena
Who endured the many months of my absence from the family.

Table of Contents

Introduction

Storytelling has been around since the beginning of time. Stories told and adventures lived are the basis of countless books that are loved by millions of people. While being passed from person to person, stories can inform and entertain, change a belief, and offer a new perspective.

Whether as fact or fiction, or as song or poem, stories can provide a glimpse into the past, present or future while entertaining the reader. Stories catapult the reader into another time and place and allow the reader to hear, taste, touch, smell and see the experience through the mind's eye.

As time goes by, it seems, it is harder to put everything down on paper in such a way as to hold the reader captive; to make the reader want to keep reading and find out what's coming next. Sure , it may seem to be an easy task to think of a funny, exciting or memorable experience where you are familar with the whole picture. But the hard part of storytelling is to reproduce that picture in detail and paint that picture with words, so the reader can experience and enjoy it.

I have written a few stories that tell of past things that have stuck in my mind. These stories are the things that I have done, things that others around me have done, and the fun that I have had telling of these adventures.

So come along with me on my journey and let me spin a tale of humor and adventure. This story is just a small window into which you can look and see, in your mind, the seafaring adventures and sights that have been written for you to enjoy.

Chapter 1

Captain
Ace

I t was by pure accident and not really my fault either that after years of working as a deckhand on charter boats, commercial boats and also being a captain of almost any other small craft that floated, I received the moniker of "ACE" one year while on an excursion in Alaska. Working long hours and months of being away from family and friends trying to scratch out a living from the waters of the ocean was an experience that most people would pass up for a more suitable job that would keep them at home.

I had been dreaming of going to Alaska and working the abundant waters that could ensure me a nice amount of money to which I could return home and relax for several months and live off those wages. I had taken a job as a boat captain in Dillingham, Alaska for a company that operated on a shoestring. The boats were of world war two vintage that were used for transporting fish from the fishermen to the processing plant that was located on shore. The hours were long and the work was hard having to endure no sleep and the wrath of the other fishermen when things didn't go as good as they expected they should. In Bristol Bay, Alaska the tides and currents are of great height and velocity. The shallow bottom constantly changes with sandbars appearing and disappearing constantly causing navigation of a small craft to be a real challenge. Lucky for me I was experienced at navigating waters where the rip tides and shallows were a constant factor. Having to know where the deep water was and where to stay away from was a learned experience.

I had been the proud owner of a small commercial boat when I was fourteen years old and had fished the area around Neah Bay, Washington and on the ocean for many years learning from the other fishermen who had been fishing there for a lifetime. The years of working on boats and learning the rules of the road paid off when I went in and passed the test to get my Captain's license. Some time later after being a charter boat captain and still fishing a commercial boat for salmon and bottom fish, I got my chance to skipper a fish buying boat in Alaska.

During the first year of my tenure as captain of that fish buying tender, the big strike over prices occurred in Bristol Bay that all but shut down the fishing industry that year there. For most fishermen and the companies that bought the fish, the season was a bust. Very few fish were being caught bought or sold. It was a dismal situation that had a bitter end waiting for all concerned that made their living off the industry.

Early the next year in February, I decided to take a job as a deckhand on board a two hundred-foot processing ship. Even though I had my captain's license and could have skippered other boats, I felt it would be a good experience for me to get my feet wet on a large ship. Needless to say getting your feet wet is an understatement. On a large ship of that kind and nature one must run before learning how to walk. It is pretty much a dead run from the moment you step foot aboard a processing ship.

I had gotten up very early the morning I was to leave on a flight out of Seattle, Washington bound for Anchorage, Alaska. The time zone difference sets you back an hour by the time you arrive there. And that's after five hours of being thoroughly bored having to endure the cramped quarters of a jet plane. After landing in Anchorage, I still had to catch another flight and journey farther west to Kodiak Island. I wasn't lucky enough to just be staying in Anchorage for the day or overnight. I had to hop another plane after trying to recover from that nightmare they call the friendly skies. So I had to make a mad dash through the airport to catch my next flight out of Anchorage. I looked like O.J. Simpson leaping over baggage, chairs and little kids that try to tackle you as you are headed for the ticket counter and your flight that is just about to leave.

When I arrived in Kodiak, Alaska I wound up having a four-hour lay over till the next flight left for a small village called Old Harbor. That was where my ship was located. Old Harbor is a little village about sixty miles down island of Kodiak that sits on the southern coast of Kodiak Island. It is also located in the middle of the Kodiak game refuge where of course there are lots of Kodiak brown bears. It's quite a sight to see people waiting in their trucks at the garbage dump to dump their garbage because of four or five big brownies that have decided to stop in for dinner. The village people just wait till the bears are finished then they throw out more treats for them to eat. Every now and then one of the bears gets a little too curious and wanders off down the main street of town. The local bear patrol gets a call and they go out in their armored truck and chase the bear back up into the woods.

I arrived by bush plane in Old Harbor about ten hours after I left Seattle. As the small plane flew over the mountains and the town of Old Harbor came into view, I could see the ship sitting alongside the one and only pier that extended out from the shore in the middle of town. My first view of the ship as we made our decent was one of the questions that got answered right away. She was fairly large, almost the size of a football field in length. She was a converted cargo ship that had been refitted for processing crab, herring and salmon. It looked like a big, black steel hulk but was still able to perform all the duties it was intended to do. She had a large, white processing house on her main deck just forward of the wheelhouse that covered one third of the deck forward of the main house. On top of the processing house were two small knuckle-boom cranes. On her forward deck in front of the processing house stood two seventy-foot tall king posts that housed the cable drums and the huge boom arms for the main ships gear used for lifting cargo. On each side of the white processing house was her name-Denali, the original name of Alaska's highest mountain.

The pilot woke me out of my trance by telling me to "hold on, we're going in for the landing." I looked out the window of the plane in time to see a small, dirt path that he said was the runway. I figured since he had done this before a few times that he knew what he was doing and in fact that was an actual runway. He swung the plane hard over to port, then straightened her out as I tried to swallow my stomach back down into its approiate place. He then cut power and we dropped like a flat rock pulling her up just before touching down on that dirt path. "Well here we are," he said, smiling as though he expected me to tip him. I unfolded myself as I crawled out of that winged coffin and felt like kissing the ground. As I turned away from him and surveyed my surroundings, I could feel the blood slowly returning to the vital parts of my body. The pilot had unloaded a few boxes of cargo that was in the plane and not seeing my two sea bags, I asked him where my bags were. He had a look of total amazement on his face. "Bags? What bags? He said. Then like a pre-recorded voice he said that he would check with the airlines when he got back to Kodiak. I thanked him for the wonderful flight and headed off in the direction of the ship.

As I made my way through the streets of Old Harbor, I could see women and children staring at me through the windows of their houses as I passed by. At least I didn't have to carry my sea bags being as tired as I was at that moment. As I walked down the old wooden dock toward the Denali, I could hear the machinery on board running and see several of the crew walking around the main deck dressed in rain gear. To get on board the ship I had to climb what is known as a "Jacob's ladder". This is a ladder that is made from line and wooden boards and is hung over the side of the ship from the main deck. Now I was really glad I didn't have my sea bags to haul up that ladder with me. As I made it to the main deck, I could see that the galley was located in the aft section of the main house. I walked along the steel deck past a few of the crew's quarters and upon entering the galley I did a double take. There standing at the end of a food bar with eight stools stood a man; well he was really two men squeezed into one body. He was about six feet tall and six feet around. He wore an apron that was almost black with grease and tied around his chest. He smiled a big Cheshire cat smile with eyes that twinkled in that big round face of his. I said, "Hi, I'm Gary, I'm the new deckhand." His smile got even bigger as he rolled his huge body around the bar and walked toward me. "I'm Bob, the cook, glad to meet you" he said. He was a behemoth on two legs, how they kept him standing is still a mystery to me. He had to have gone four hundred and fifty pounds give or take a few pounds. I asked him whom I was supposed to see to get myself squared away on board. He pointed the way to the wheelhouse where he said the processing manager should be.

I climbed the gangway to the upper deck where there were more crew quarters and the wheelhouse. I walked into the wheelhouse and introduced myself. The processing manager Ron, the secretary Susan, and the ship's other deckhand Alan warmly welcomed me. The wheelhouse was a beautiful place with varnished wood, a large chart table against the rear wall, two raised seats, electronics, a four foot diameter wheel and a brass, ship's telegraph to engineering. A telegraph is a round brass post with a larger round face on the top of it. It has several sections on the face that have different orders written on them. The orders in each section of the face were different. They ranged from "Full Astern" to "Full Ahead" with a section in the twelve o'clock position that read "All Stops." Attached to the face of the telegraph was a two-handled piece of brass that had a small rectangular window on each handle in front of the faces of the telegraph that showed which order the captain wanted. In the engineering section where the huge engine was, there was another one similar to the one in the wheelhouse. When the captain wanted the ship to go ahead one half speed, he would grab the handle of the telegraph and shove it back and forth a few times stopping on the section he wanted the engine set at. The telegraph in engineering had a loud ringer in it that they could hear, then seeing where the captain stopped the handle; they could set the speed of the engine appropriately.

The wood was trimmed in brass and alongside the door was a haws pipe. A haws pipe is a long, brass pipe that goes from the wheelhouse down to the engine room. The captain to talk to the engineer uses this. The top end has a curved opening with a spring-loaded cover piece with a hole in the middle of it. The captain puts his mouth inside the curved piece and blows real hard. The cover piece with the hole is a whistle and can be heard above the engine's noise in the engine room. The captain then pushes the cover open and hears the engineer answer. This is how they talk to one another when underway.

14

After filling out the necessary paperwork I got asked if I was ready to go to work. I told them that my sea bags were somewhere between here and Seattle, but sure why not get started. Alan said that he had an extra coat and a watch cap I could use till my sea bags caught up with me. We ventured out on top of the processing house to where the two knuckle-boom cranes were. Alan gave me a crash course on what each lever did and the signals that are used when loading and unloading cargo. He also said that there was a cargo ship coming to off load equipment for us real soon. And no sooner than the words hit my ears I looked out over the water and saw a large ship approaching from the east. "There she is" he said. We got her tied fast along side us and after a quick battle plan was decided upon on how to get everything off the cargo ship, onto our ship and onto the dock so that it could be taken to a warehouse; we started in. We worked all night and half the next day transferring cargo. Now about thirty hours later since I had my last bout of sleep, I was starting to get a little tired needless to say. We did get a few breaks with meals every six hours apart where I could hook up an I.V. of coffee to keep myself going.

Later that next afternoon my sea bags finally caught up with me. I wondered if they got the nice relaxing lay over that escaped me the day before. After unloading that ship of her cargo some thirty-six hours later since I left Seattle, I was in need of a little sleep. I grabbed a bunk in one of the modular sleeping units that was located on the upper deck, threw my sea bags on the bunk and crawled into bed with them.

The next day started at 0500 with another I.V. hook up of coffee and breakfast, then it was off to work operating the ship's gear or working the processing line. We worked an average of eighteen hours a day unloading boats and processing what is known as Tanner crab. Several years ago a large restaurant chain started buying Tanner crab. They figured out that people would not like the name and so being enterprising people, they probably hired and over paid some advertising person that gave that bland, soft, no taste shellfish the name-Snow Crab. Of course! Snow! White, fluffy, pure pretty, etc., etc.

What a marketing scheme it was. But I guess it wasn't good enough because that restaurant chain went out of business some years later. That advertising person is probably writing jingles for toilet paper now.

During the first two weeks of working eighteen-hour days in the freezing snow and wind, I got to know the whole ship and her crew. My partner Alan, the other deckhand was known as the "Wookie." About all you could see of his face were his nose, eyes, and a little skin of his cheeks. The rest was hair, long, brown, rough hair. Every now and then you could see his mouth when he was yelling at someone telling them how intelligent they were. He had two attitudes that ranged from bad to worse. I don't know if I impressed him with my intelligence at first or if it was the fact that I was the new guy and he had to see if I was worth my salt or not before he would start on me. Apparently I found out later that he had told the manager and the captain (who had not flown in yet) that I was OK and was doing a good job. That was until that fateful day.

About the end of the second week on board ship, I was pretty comfortable with all the workings of the ship. I had spent long hours learning everything by doing it; sort of trial by fire to test my metal. One day when I was operating the starboard side crane on top of the processing house, I had a tote full of equipment hanging off the end of a fully extended boom in front of the house. A tote is a four foot by four foot by four foot deep box that is used for holding fish, guts, garbage, equipment and people. When full of stuff they can weigh up to two thousand pounds. Nothing you'd want dropped on your toe. I was watching and waiting for signals from the "Wookie" down on the main deck as he and a few of the crew were working on a project. That was one thing we never ran out of-projects. We had a project for everything. Hell we even had a project to set up and do a project. As I was standing there being frozen solid as a Popsicle, I got a signal from someone down on the main deck. I didn't see whom it was that gave the signal, but it was a hand in the air that I could see just above the edge of the roofline. It was a "thumbs down" signal-the signal to lower the boom. So lower it I did. Talk about a quick response, I had people jumping up and down and running to get out of the way. The stream of obscenities that came along with the stampede of people from the main deck cannot be put into print.

Nothing like a little surprise finding out that a slight miscommunication coupled along with a mechanical malfunction could be so much fun to watch. Of course from my vantage point of not being able to see all that happened, I can only guess as to the quickness of some of the crew running for their lives.

Well that was all it took for the "Wookie" to come unglued. He called me every name in the book. I'd like to see that book just to see if there are that many names in it. Finally after taking a breath he announced, "You know, I'm going to call you "Ace." Because when you do everything right, you do it perfect, and when you screw up, you screw up perfect."

Of course there was nothing that I could say or do to defend myself against their beliefs and the mechanical failure of the crane due to the hydraulics skipping a beat and having a brain fart. When we checked the crane out afterwards it worked fine. To this day I still think that that piece of steel was possessed and had it in for me.

But from that day forward I was known as "Ace." The "Wookie" told everyone that was my name. He wouldn't tell anybody why; just to call me "Ace." During the several months that I was on board ship, people came and went and every one of them never knew my real name. I always had people ask me what my real name was but after so long of being up there and everybody else just calling me "Ace" I figured why complicate the issue; I didn't tell them either.

So to this day the name of "Captain Ace" has stayed the course. In the beginning I tried to avoid the new name but it did no good. I was swimming against a strong tide and was losing ground, so I decided to swim with it and accept it. In the years to come the name did help me to some extent when others in the business who knew me from that time remembered the name. I must have made an impression of some sort on whomever because it served me well in having the right people in the business remember me. I was never without an offer to work for someone in Alaska.

Chapter 2

The Wookie

For those of you that are Star Wars fans and know who the Wookie is, I should have no problem in describing Alan who had been the deck hand on the Denali for the past two years. He was a good-sized guy at about six feet two inches tall and tipped the scales at two hundred and thirty pounds. He was not in great shape as far as being a muscular man but he was strong. The one thing he did have was hair. He was a very hairy guy. No wonder he could stand around out in sub zero tempetures with just a T-shirt on and not be cold. He had his own fur coat to keep him warm.

His entire face was just about covered with hair too. His beard was about four inches long that covered his face to the point that all you could see was just a bit of skin of his cheeks that joined his dark eyes. When talking to him and if it was something he liked or was in a semi-good mood (which wasn't often) his eyes twinkled as if he were hiding the greatest secret ever. I always wondered what scheme he was planning or what devious plan he had up his sleeve when I worked with him which was just about all the time.

He also had long hair that looked like a fisherman's reel that just backlashed and had the biggest bird's nest in it that you can get from back lashing. About the only thing you can do with it is cut it all out and start over from scratch.

The Wookie had two attitudes that ranged from bad to worse. He used them to his advantage on board ship to keep people away from him. He had gotten the position by his working knowledge of the ship and all that went on. He had come up through the ranks from being a grungy processor learning how to be in the right place at the right time learning the ropes of the ship and using a little bit of ingenuity to get the job.

His persistence at hanging around and probably bugging the hell out of people made an impression on the skipper who gave him the job just to keep him under wraps and at least have a say in what and how he did things. Although the skipper was a well-known commodity among the Alaskan fleet of tenders and processors, he was known to be a pirate when dealing with certain things.

The Wookie, sometimes by whatever method fit the occasion was adept at being underhanded, schemeful, sometimes mean but always aware of his surroundings when he set his mind to a project. He too was a pirate in the sense of having to improvise on several occasions to acquire the necessary equipment that was needed in times of want. He always had a smile on his face when doing business with some poor plant operator or fisherman who hadn't a clue to his motives for procuring items of interest. His method of operation was that of a shark on the hunt of an easy prey. His best-loved saying to his credit was "Trust me." He even advertised the fact by wearing a hat that said the same thing.

When I used to get into a conversation with him and a question came up as to the validity of something, he would stop talking to me and just point at his hat and smile that big Cheshire cat grin. I wonder how many times he watched Alice in Wonderland when he was a kid?

At first when I met him and started working along side him he was pretty business like in his dealings with me and not too friendly as to want to invite me into his complete confidence. That's sometimes the case with a lot of people, they are a little standoffish at first until they get to know you. Of course I was my usual jovial self which probably made him sick just talking to me. But somehow I must have grown on him to a point that he knew he wasn't going to get rid of me that easy and also of the fact that I was stranded on board that ship with him for six months. Believe me when I say it was a challenge for me to get under his skin as to let him know that I myself was somewhat of a pirate too and that his bullshit didn't really impress me or intimidate me. As the old saying goes, you can't bullshit an old bullshitter.

It really didn't take long before he realized that I was not a green horn that just fell off the turnip truck and happened to wind up there not knowing a thing. It was just after the first few times of the two of us getting into arguments that we both found out how much fun we were having feeding off each other.

During the time when we were buried up to our necks in work, if something happened that was wrong or was something that made us stop work, we would start an argument with each other. The bell sounded and it was no holds barred when it came to the insults, profanity and anything else we could think of at that time.

"Go piss up a rope!" I'd yell at him. And the term, "Blow it out your ass" was a popular phrase that was also used. The reply to that ingenious phrase would be "I did and you came out" was a standard saying that was sort of the ground work by which all other insults and profanities were measured by. The stream of profanities would continue until we couldn't think of another one to use on each other without repeating ourselves. That would be a very bad thing for either one of us to do. To repeat an insult or use a profanity in the same session would be degrading on us and would show a lack of intelligence.

All work stopped and the rest of the crew would just stand there with their mouths hanging open staring at us as we were going at it verbally. We never got physical as to start a donnybrook onboard but everybody who was in earshot of us would of thought it was coming. At the end of our little conversation, we would both stop yelling at each other and looking at each other with satisfaction, we would both break out in hysterical laughter. Everybody had to of thought we were out of our minds as to go on for several minutes insulting, cursing and yelling at each other only to end it in such a way as to make them all feel like they'd been had. And actually they had been had. We mainly did that for their benefit just to see the reaction we'd get from the crew who were not in on the joke.

The Wookie and I had somehow come to the realization and understanding that we knew we were both full of shit and that it didn't do any good to try and outdo the other with vast knowledge and showmanship of it. So we would just put it on display for all to try and see if they could figure it out. That was the great part of the entire time that we were captive on board ship, that the two of us now had an accomplice to work things out easier. The more schemes and tricks one or the other could come up with the better. One of our favorite little schemes was one of shear delight and admiration on our part.

When the ship was underway and we were headed for a particular harbor or port of call, many times the ship had to anchor out in the bay because there were no docks or piers to tie up to. And of course being a large ship doesn't afford you the ease of just pulling up to a dock and lowering the gangway down for comfort of coming and going. So it was essential that we had to use the anchor quite often.

The anchor and anchor chain for a large ship is in itself quite large too. The ship's gear used to pull the anchor had to be run off the main hydraulic system, so the anchor winch was large and powerful also. When hoisting the anchor up off the bottom, the anchor chain, with each link being about an inch thick, eight inches long and having a center piece welded in each link had to travel up through the hull, over the winch and down into the chain locker. The chain locker was a completely sealed room with no lights. The room was about ten feet by ten feet with a large steel bin in the middle of it where the chain had to be coiled up by a crewman upon bringing it in.

There were only two ways in and out of that room. One was by a small hatch cover that was located in the ceiling of the chain locker that was connected to one of the lower decks. That was where a crewman would enter the chain locker to coil the chain as it came down from the winch. The other way in and out of the locker was a hatch door that was located on the aft portion of the locker behind the bin that was connected to the food storage cage on the other side of a main bulkhead. Nobody else beside the skipper and a few select people knew of this hatchway.

After assessing the crew and deciding on who would be a good prospect to put on their rain gear and go down into the chain locker, the Wookie and I went to work. We would start telling stories and talking about the chain locker beast saying how we have been trying to kill it for the past year, how it gets into the food storage area by way of holes it had put in the bulkhead. The beast had somehow mutated into a big, hairy thing with glowing eyes because of the chemicals it got into a long time ago. We had seen it a few times and that it resembled a huge rat that wasn't afraid of anything. We told our story of how we couldn't shoot it because of the steel walls, that a bullet might ricochet off a wall and hit us and a rat trap might be big enough for one of it's feet because he was so big.

We were like boy scout leaders sitting around a campfire with wide eyed kids all around us hanging on each word not really sure whether to believe us or not.

Days before the anchor was to be hoisted we would implore the help of the processing foreman to help us out on our quest for fun and the ultimate goal of scaring the living daylights out of our victim. When we were to hoist the anchor we made sure that our crewman was there and that he was assigned the task of coiling the anchor chain. We would tell him how the chain was to be coiled when it came down through the deck pipe and also to watch out for the locker beast because it liked fresh meat and could smell him down in there. We told him to work fast and get out of there when he was done.

He would get his rain gear and his gloves on and climb down into the chain locker to await the inevitable task of coiling that big, heavy chain while cramped up in that chain bin. The only light in the chain locker was from the open hatchway about two feet above his head.

Before he would go into the chain locker, we made sure that he saw all of us standing around on deck so as not to be wondering where any of us were at not being present so as to give the plan away or draw suspicion on any one of us. As he made his way down to the lower deck, the Wookie would go another way and be in the chain locker before the foreman got the signal from him. The Wookie would be in place having gone through the other hatchway door dressed in a hairy mask with green glow in the dark eyes. It looked like a cheap holloween costume in the daylight but down in that totally dark room it looked great.

I would be operating the anchor winch hauling the chain up out of the water and letting it run down the pipe into the locker at a slow speed. When the anchor was at the waterline, I would signal our foreman with a stop and start of the winch. The anchor still had to travel another fifty feet to come up tight against the ship.

The man at the hatch door would then slam it shut and lock it. With just a few more feet of chain creeping in through the pipe and the noise it made, the Wookie could move around easily. The beast would pop it's head up over the chain bin for a quick second looking around the room then drop back down behind the bin. It would then reappear in another place and start to make a growling noise loud enough for the crewman to hear. The beast would be scratching at the metal on the bin with an old turkey bone, which would be dropped into the bin with the chain and the crewman.

By this time when the winch stopped, I could hear muffled screaming and some banging going on down below that was coming from the chain locker. It sounded like something out of an old time horror movie. The foreman would then open the hatch door where upon the crewman would almost fly straight up out of the locker. The guy looked as though he had seen a ghost. The Wookie by this time had made his way back out of the chain locker and dumped his costume. He joined me on the upper deck and just gave me that smile that let me know we succeeded. The foreman and the crewman would come up the elevator to the main weather deck where the Wookie and I were standing.

The crewman would proceed to yell and swear and tell us that there was something down there in the chain locker. That he saw an ugly, hairy thing with glowing eyes that almost came after him.

25

He said that whatever it was, it scared the shit out of him. He also wanted to know how the hell the hatch door got closed too.

The foreman told him that he didn't know how it got closed, that he had to go to the blast freezer to check on something and it must of got closed somehow by itself. The Wookie and I played dumb. As we were standing there we could smell something strange. I moved around the winch and stood next to the crewman who was still ranting and raving about the beast. It smelled like urine; this guy came out of there and realized that he had literally pissed his pants. It was very obvious to him and us by the smell and the fact that he wanted to rush off and get away from us. His face was pretty white and he had a look of total embarrassment too. We kept asking him what happened but he didn't elaborate on it too much. He hurried off in the direction of the bunkhouse to get away from us.

After the Wookie and I got the winch secured and decided to take a break, we were sitting in the galley a short time later when that crewman came down from the bunkhouse. Both of us noticed that he was now wearing black colored jeans instead of blue jeans.

The Wookie and I asked him why he changed his pants after coming out of the chain locker. To this the crewman called us a few words that cannot be repeated here that related to the origins of our birth, grabbed a cup of coffee and exited the galley as the entire galley erupted into laughter.

Chapter 3

THE
MECCA

Located in the Gulf of Alaska where some of the worst storms in the Pacific Ocean are born lies Kodiak Island. Kodiak Island is not quite at the end of the world, but in the city of Kodiak they say you can see it from there. Kodiak is home to one of the largest fleet of commercial fishing boats that venture out into the ocean. Herring, salmon, bottomfish and crab are the primary targets of the incredibly brave men who travel many miles to bring in their catch to earn a living. Any man would be half crazy, if not all, to earn a living battling rough, high seas, howling winds and sub-zero temperatures.

I have been on that fine line that divides one's sanity when you come to the realization from working twenty or thirty hours on a boat that could take you down and be swallowed up by the sea in a matter of minutes. You are taking a risk every day just being out there working for that living. It is considered the most dangerous job in the world with deaths occurring on a regular basis, and the men who do this job know it. Many precautions are taken to try and keep everybody alive and well while working in these conditions.

When the long hours of work are just about over and you have been beaten to death from the seemingly endless pitching and rolling boat in the rough seas, you finally see the fish hold is just about full. Full of the bounty you have worked so hard and long for. Seeing that is a wonderful sight because you know it is time to turn the boat toward shore and head for the dock to unload your precious cargo. By this time you don't care about the twenty-five foot seas or the sixty-knot gusts of wind you're battling — you're headed for dry ground.

After enduring many days on rough seas, feeling like a Dixie cup in a washing machine, there is a place in Kodiak where a salty dog can get some much-needed rest and relaxation in a way most normal people would not consider safe or sane. But remember, we aren't dealing with normal people here. Some of these guys are a few clowns short of a full circus, and the one place they go to put their craziness on display is a place called "The Mecca." The Mecca is their true goal, their final stop after all the fish or crab have been offloaded and sold, the boat is tied fast to the dock and they have a fistful of money to do with what they will.

When you still have your wits about you, the basic necessities of life are thought of for a brief second. But items such as new clothes, toiletries, boots or good rain gear are soon dismissed as unnecessary evils that would diminish your hard-earned cache of treasure to the point of having to limit your spending power for rest and relaxation.

God forbid that would ever happen to someone who has cheated death time and again by surviving yet another battle with the elements. Although, killing a few million brain cells and drinking yourself into a total stupor is not considered life threatening by any means, at least not by a crazy sea dog's standards.

The Mecca is a catchall for anyone who is looking for that one particular place that can be their source of fun, entertainment and excitement — like having your ass sucking seat covers in a major storm thirty miles from shore isn't enough excitement for you?

It is a cross between a nightclub and a first avenue wino's bar. It has a unique dÈcor that reminds you of a turn of the century saloon with old relics of ship's gear and gaudy art on the beer stained walls. It is a large place that has a stage for the various live bands that just happen to make their way out toward the end of the world, and a wooden dance floor big enough for about three dozen drunk people to hop around the floor like wounded deer. But then again, nobody really cares if you dance like you have snowshoes on either. There are a few small tables around the dance floor area with some cozy booths against the walls.

On the far side of the room is the bar. It is a large horseshoe-shaped bar with old wooden bar stools that have been glued back together numerous times from previous melees between two salts who might have had differing opinions while visiting that fine establishment.

The Mecca is a gathering spot for some to come and share their experiences of years past when their boats would overflow with fish and crab. Of days gone by when it was a relished dream and a reality of making a fine living from the sea.

When a sailor has salt water in his veins, there is nothing that he loves more than the sea. He takes the good with the bad and keeps on doing what he loves to do best. Many a days you can see the old salts sitting around the bar drinking beer and telling sea stories of past adventures out on the ocean.

The Mecca is the place where a person can get what is known as "Mecca-nized." On most nights in the Mecca there are quite a few of the regulars that come in to do business. They are there to make a little extra spending money. These are the people that have taken a liking to the fact that most of the salty dogs, when half in the bag, will be looking for certain items of interest. Everything from fishing gear to contraband is bartered in the booths that line the walls.

In Alaska, all items are high priced. If the government invested in selling everything from food to clothing in Alaska, they could pay off the national debt in just a few years. Nothing is cheap.

That being said, the Mecca is also a place that services what it sells. For someone who isn't that knowledgeable of the services offered at this fine establishment, one of the oldest services known to man can be obtained there also. If you are so inclined to partake of them, you need to have a few dollars in your pocket.

These are the working girls that make it their occupational duty to service the salty dogs that have been out to sea for a long time. When the urge arises (no pun intended) and you have the money (to the tune of two hundred dollars for one-half hour of fun), you can take advantage of the fine services that await you.

Another very fine show that is offered at the Mecca is table dancing. A few of the girls there accomplish a great deal of exercise dancing on some tables in the rear of the bar. Although table dancing is supposed to take place on top of the table, the under-the-table dancing is also popular sometimes. Even though there were special places for that kind of service, some guys elected to delve into the debauchery of the uninhibited.

My crew and I knew these beautiful women who worked at the Mecca and had become good friends with them. We would drink, dance and just have a good time without doing "business" with them. It was rumored that our first mate had weakened during a drunken stupor and was seen walking away with one of the girls to the "business" room, but nobody would admit to it.

The Wookie and I would go about our own unique way of trying to set up one of the innocent and naive crew members so he would never forget his last night in Kodiak. Upon entering the Mecca the day before we were to set sail for Cordova, we had devised a plan to get one of our innocent greenhorn crew members some special services. We took up a collection from the rest of the crew by telling them it was this one guy's birthday. Even though his birthday wasn't for another three months, nobody knew the difference. We just about got all the money that was needed for him to have a good time with one of the girls there at the Mecca, but we lacked a few dollars for the full meal deal.

Since we were friends with the girls there at the bar, we promised them a return on their services provided for in the future. That did the trick for procuring a negotiated settlement with one of the girls who must have been a little short of cash.

The Wookie and I just about exhausted all of the reasons in the world why our crewman should come with us for the last celebration in Kodiak that night. He didn't want to go. He kept telling us that he didn't have enough money. He finally gave in when the Wookie said that "we" would buy him drinks (words I thought I'd never hear come out of his mouth). At that moment I wondered if I was hearing voices or if some alien had taken over the Wookie's mind. I gave him that look of intrigue that said, "What the hell are you talking about!?" There was no answer that could be given at that point since the damage had already been done.

The Wookie and I put our little plan into action that night with the help of the barmaid spiking his drink. The girls did a table dance for him that almost put him under the table. We had to hold him up to keep him from sliding down onto the floor. After a few hours of some heavy drinking, we grabbed him up and packed him off to one of the "business" rooms in back of the building where our guy was taken advantage of by the girl we paid off.

31

Somehow a lot of pictures were taken of the whole affair and wound up plastered on the walls of the galley a couple of days later.

The party went on til the next morning when the Kodiak harbor police finally wandered into the bar and informed the owner that it was time to close her up for the night. That happened at around five in the morning when there were just a few of the diehards left that hadn't spent all their money on wine, women and song.

It was really a shame that it had to end so soon. But after a couple of days of trying to kill as many brain cells as possible and crawling back to the ship on your hands and knees (stopping along the way to empty the contents of your stomach) and realizing the fact that you are now flat broke, you tell yourself over and over that you're never going to do that again … at least not until the next time you hit port with a fistful of money.

As we sailed out of Kodiak that next day, making our way out of the channel between Kodiak Island and Near Island, past dozens of eagles sitting in the tree tops waiting for the processing plants to start grinding fish and dumping the fish waste out in the channel, we headed east for the open waters of the Pacific.

Another island just east of Kodiak Island is Afognak Island. On this island are several houses that stand just above the beach along the channel. As we made our way past those houses, out on the deck of one of them stood three beautiful, naked ladies who were all waving goodbye to us as the ship made her way past their house.

As the fight for the binoculars erupted inside the wheelhouse, the skipper gave one loud, long blast on the ship's horn. He was letting them hear our good-byes also as we headed out. With that visual and our aching heads, we knew then that more good times were to be had by all on our return trip to the Mecca.

Chapter 4

ICEBERGS IN THE STORM

Weather in Alaska has a mind of it's own. It's fickle, stubborn, and unpredictable — and can be very dangerous. It can be a nice day out on the water where it seems like you couldn't have a care in the world. The boat is making way along a preset course headed for a certain destination where all the timetables have been interpolated as to allow for winds and current. The position of the ship is carefully plotted every half-hour and in limited visibility the radar is checked constantly for land and any other ships that might be in the area.

The radios blare with the weather reports of each particular area around the entire northern pacific and the Bering Sea. You listen for the area that you are in and where you are headed to see if you're going to have to take shelter somewhere to avoid the onslaught of a fierce storm that may be predicted. Although the weather reports are somewhat accurate, there is that degree of the unknown that raises the hair on the back of your neck and tells you all is not right. That feeling is one which an old salt has come to rely on to keep himself and his crew alive.

But there are times when even that sixth sense can fail you and you are caught in that battle of the elements where it is you against a very nasty storm. The saying "If you don't like the weather, wait fifteen minutes, it'll change" always seems to apply to the negative aspect when you're thirty miles from the nearest sheltered cove or port. Any port in a storm will do when faced with that kind of choice. It really doesn't take a rocket scientist or a lawyer to figure that one out.

When traversing the Gulf of Alaska, it is a crapshoot as to whether you are going to get lucky and avoid any foul weather. Either the water is fairly calm and the winds are light, or you are going to get the snot bubbles kicked out of you by fifty- or sixty-knot winds and twenty-five-foot walls of water that break and curl over the bow of the boat.

It is times like those that make you seriously ask yourself, "What the hell am I doing out here?" The thoughts of being at home sitting in front of a warm fire with a nice hot cup of cocoa seem to replay in your mind as you fight the continuous pounding and the curling walls of water that cover your boat in green water. Everywhere you look all you can see is white caps on top of the waves and the saltwater spray from the wind. The tops of the waves are being blown off, causing a white streak of foam to appear on the water in between each wave. It is a place that is not fit for man or beast to be in.

As our ship headed east out of Kodiak harbor and into the Gulf of Alaska, the crew was busy getting the ship ready for the five day journey to Prince William Sound and our final destination of Cordova. There is always work to be done when getting under way. The main ship's gear must be lashed down and secured in such a way as to prevent the huge crane boom arms from breaking loose and swinging wildly if a storm were to suddenly come upon us.

The boom arms are laid down on the top of the processing house and the thick, heavy cables are paid out and wrapped around the two smaller knuckle-boom cranes. The cables are crossed back across each arm to the opposite boom arm where they are brought up tight against each other creating a solid hold on each arm.

The boom winches are locked in place with a large, steel marlinespike so they would not bleed off and the cable couldn't loosen up causing the boom-arms to move. All barrels, processing equipment and anything that could come loose was lashed down with chain binders or line. All the mooring lines were secured to the railings and everyone had to have their quarters secured also. This was a basic routine that was carried out whenever the ship sailed.

During the first day after we plotted our course that would take us into the southern entrance of Prince William Sound, the weather was as nice as it could get for that part of the Alaskan Gulf. The seas were a mere six feet and the winds were fifteen knots out of the northeast.

My on-duty time in the wheelhouse consisted of two six-hour shifts that were split. I would work six hours on duty at the helm steering the ship, then be off for six hours (sometimes getting sleep), then back at the helm again for another six hours.

The first few days while underway, the majority of the crew enjoyed some free time by playing cards, watching movies on the VCR in the galley and sleeping extra hours that are not normally there to be taken. The captain, the first mate, the engineers, the Wookie and I all kept working during this time. We had to make sure that the ship was on course and in good shape.

Of course during some of this free time the Wookie and I made it a point to continue our endeavors to pull a few tricks on some of the unsuspecting crew members.

After researching most of the crew and determining who the

next victim would be, we would agree on a likely victim and tell him that he needed to help us do some work in the fidley. The fidley is the long, vertical shaft area that houses the exhaust pipes from all the engines in the engine room. In the engine room there was the main powerful Fairbanks-Morse six-cylinder train engine. She had pistons a yard wide and was over twenty feet long and ten feet tall. On both sides of the main engine were the diesel generator engines: two, six-cylinder Detroit's that were used to power the lights and various other small equipment; one twelve-cylinder Detroit which powered the ammonia freezing; and the big sixteen-cylinder Detroit diesel that powered the four blast freezers. She could blast freeze over one hundred thousand pounds of salmon in a twenty-four hour period and the hold could keep one and a half million pounds of product at a cool minus fifteen degrees Fahrenheit in storage before offloading to the buyers.

The fidley had two ladders and two small walkways that allowed access to all the pipes. The Wookie and I would have our unsuspecting crewman/victim sit in a bosun's chair, then hoist him high into the top of the fidley by the hauling line. A bosun's chair is a flat piece of wood with a line attached to each side of the seat, which is attached to a long line used with a pulley to hoist a person up or lower them down over the side of a ship.

We gave him a brush and a bucket and told him that the pipes in the top of the exhaust area had to be cleaned due to health rules. After we hoisted the crewman high into the fidley, we tied the hauling line off on one of the ladders, leaving him suspended at the top of the fidley. We told him to wait for us while we went and blew the pipes out. Even though the engines were already running and there was no such job to be done, it sounded good at the time.

Having an unsuspecting crewman stranded at the top of the fidley (the highest point on the ship), while the ship was under way and rocking back and forth and up and down, was an opportunity we just couldn't pass up. We knew this particular crewman would most likely get sick … and it didn't take long to hear the results of our little scheme. The Wookie and I stood just outside the hatchway door and heard him start yelling at the top of his lungs for someone to come and get him down. "Hey!!! Somebody get me the hell out of here, I'm gonna puke all over the place!"

No one else could hear him yelling over the sound of the engines. "Do you think he puked yet?" I asked. "

"Well if he does, he has a bucket with him; just hope he uses It." the Wookie said.

After listening to the retching and gagging for a minute or two, the Wookie and I stepped back into the fidley and asked him how he was doing. He responded with a very loud and sorrowful wail. He pleaded with us to get him down from up there and informed us that he had just puked in his bucket and he was sick.

The Wookie and I smiled at each other with that knowing look of success having pulled off another one of our little capers. We proceeded to lower him back down to the walkway we were standing on. Once on the walkway, the Wookie growled at him to get his ass out of there and take his bucket of puke with him and clean it out. The Wookie had a lot of sympathy for his fellow crewmen.

After the guy ran off carrying his bucket of puke with him, the Wookie and I slowly strolled back to the wheelhouse to plot our next mischievous prank.

On the last day of traveling across the gulf, the weather decided to take a turn for the worse. It started to blow as if Mother Nature was trying to get revenge on us.

The radio in the wheelhouse splashed out the details of a storm that was brewing out on the Gulf Stream. We could have told them that it was already here. The weather had turned into a nasty monster in a matter of hours during the afternoon. The winds increased to fifty knots and the seas had built in height to about twenty feet. As we plowed into the waves, taking green water over the bow of the ship the nor'easter continued to assault us as we slowed to almost a crawl. The ship was barely making seven knots as the wind tried it's best to stop us from reaching our destination. As the storm blew the tops off the waves and we were pelted with ice and snow, the water started to freeze on the decks. The ship had a good supply of fifty pound bags of rock salt left over from the crab season where we would cover the steps and the decks with the salt to keep them as clear as we could of ice.

As the afternoon wore on we could see the entrance to Prince William Sound slowly rising up in the distance above the white water that surrounded us. The ship was taking a beating but we knew she was tough enough to withstand this type of punishment. We adjusted our course to quarter the waves a little more so as to smooth the ride out.

The sky was an eerie, gray-steel in color with snow being blown sideways across the windows of the wheelhouse. With the visibility reduced to near zero and darkness now upon us, I had my face plastered to the radar screen making sure we didn't have an unscheduled encounter with another ship or even worse, a collision with an iceberg.

Prince William Sound is well known for the glaciers that are there. Those glaciers wind their way through the mountains carving out land just to come to an abrupt stopping point at the saltwater. The huge chunks of ice that break off the faces of those cold monsters are as big as a ten story building. They float free in the saltwater traveling dozens of miles with just their tops protruding above the surface of the water. The rest of their massive hulking body lays several feet below the surface of the water. Their azure blue colors with a white coating present an ominous coldness of their own, let alone the freezing winds and snow that are ever present during a winter storm.

As we entered the southern end of Prince William Sound, the winds had dramatically increased in velocity. Gusts of up to seventy knots were pushing our five hundred-ton vessel around like a fishing bobber. The captain, by this time had started cursing and complaining about the storm. We still had several hours' worth of travel before we reached Orca Bay and Cordova. The water was covered with chunks of ice that had broken off the faces of the glaciers in the northern part of the sound.

The ship was now being battered with huge chunks of glacier ice along with the wind and waves. The waves would pick up the smaller chunks of ice and hurl them against the side of the hull while the larger pieces would ram us as if they were torpedoes trying to blast holes through the steel hull. The sound was almost deafening and made the entire crew a little uneasy listening to the onslaught that was being thrown at us. Mother Nature was pissed all right and we were getting a good spanking.

Now being the new guy aboard this ship and being one of the main crewmembers who the captain relied upon, I was most likely just in the wrong place at the wrong time. The skipper in his infinite wisdom decided that I should be the one to guide the ship through the ice field. He had all the spark and team spirit of a college football coach that was giving his team that half-time locker room pep talk.

"Now Ace, you're the man, you're the one who has to get us through this safely," he said. "You get to be the hero; how 'bout it buddy?" he said.

In other words I get to do a job that nobody else in their right mind would even consider doing. At that moment my brain went numb and all sensible reasoning froze as solid as the ice on most of the decks. I was totally speechless and couldn't utter a word for I knew if I did open my mouth, I would say something stupid like, "You've got to be shitting me, right? Since the weather was so bad and the skipper couldn't see what was in front of the ship and we were making our way through that ice filled water that looked like a very large slushy, it was imperative that we did not end up like the Titanic hitting one of those monster chunks.

The skipper informed me that I was to go stand up on the bow of the ship taking a hand held radio with me. I was to keep in constant contact with him in the wheelhouse and to tell him where all the big icebergs were located and where to steer the ship. This seemed like an easy task at first but I soon realized that was not to be the case.

As I pondered my fate and made my way back to my quarters to add on a few more layers of clothes and a freezer suit, I figured that either I was getting a payback for some of the rotten tricks I've pulled or I just happened to be in the wrong place at the wrong time.

I put on my freezer suit, which is a very warm set of insulated coveralls that we use for working in the hold and out on deck in snowy, nasty weather. The suit was surely needed for this particular job that I was so lucky to get. I went back into the wheelhouse and grabbed a hand held radio for talking to the skipper and telling him where to steer through the icebergs.

As I was climbing down the snow-covered gangway to the main weather deck, the ship suddenly lurched forward as she hit one of those massive hulks of floating ice. Damn near all five hundred tons of steel had crawled up on a massive chunk of ice that was ninety percent under water as the ship was lifted up on a wave. When she came down she settled hard on a section of flat ice. The ship was almost as if she were aground with the bow raised up in the air and listing to starboard. The engine moaned loudly and the creaking of the ice underneath us sounded as if she was tearing a hole in her belly.

The hand held radio I was carrying came to life with the sound of the skipper screaming. He was yelling for me to get the hell up on the bow as fast as I could. I was standing only feet from the bow when all this occurred and of course the timing couldn't have been worse for me as I struggled to climb the snow-covered deck to the very peak of the bow.

I looked over the outside of the ship and saw that the ship had indeed slid up on a piece of a flat iceberg just enough to cause her to languish there for a minute. I radioed the captain and told him what was there under our bow and that we were pushing the iceberg very slowly.

Luckily the ship was going slow enough in that storm that we didn't suffer any damage. The captain was able to get the engine into reverse as quickly as possible and with the entire ship shuttering like she would break apart at any moment, slowly started to inch her way back off that chunk of ice.

As I stood up on the bow of the ship with the freezing winds howling and the waves still crashing into the ship, I could look out over the side of the ship and see the snow going upwards toward the sky instead of downwards. The winds when blowing down off the mountains at such a high speed hits the water and the side of the ship and sends the snow straight back up into the air. Most of the time the snow is traveling sideways but with seventy-feet of freeboard it creates a wall and the wind pushes the snow upwards.

In the freezing wind and water spray I kept in contact with the captain telling him where the huge icebergs were and where to steer the ship.

41

The skipper told me that we only had another hour or so to go and we would be in Orca Bay and could drop the pick. I for one was so happy to hear those words because I was almost a chunk of ice myself. I had to keep breaking the ice off of me that built up and froze on the outside of me from the spray of the waves that continued to crash into the bow of the ship.

As we wound our way through the maze of large and small icebergs, hitting only the little ones and making them bounce off the hull like we had an impenetrable shield. It seemed that we finally had stalemated Mother Nature's wrath. The storm had not gotten any worse and as far as hitting anymore monster icebergs, that was not even a possibility with my standing on the bow with a good view of them.

About two hours after the encounter with that cold, icy hulk of ice we rounded the corner on the eastern part of the sound and made our way into Orca Bay just outside Cordova.

The wind was still howling like a wild beast lost in the wilderness and the snow continued to pile up on the ship even though it appeared to be traveling upward when looking out beyond the ship.

The Wookie had donned his freezer suit and had joined me on the forward deck as we were getting ready to drop the anchor. Orca Bay was just about full of ships that were already anchored up for the night waiting out the storm. As the wind blew now more out of the east, the captain nosed the ship into a wide area away from other ships. The captain barked out over the intercom speaker that was mounted on the king post at the anchor winch that he wanted four shots of chain let out. A shot of chain is equal to ninety feet. A link of chain at that measurement is painted white so we could see it as it left the ship. As he kept the ship straight into the wind , he let her slip back slowly as we paid out the huge chain from the chain locker. I clamped down on the winch brake and yelled out the final length of chain we were at. The captain began putting pressure on the anchor by backing down on her slowly to make sure she would dig in and hold us fast to the bottom. Then he cut power to the engine and had the engineers shut her down.

The Wookie and I returned to the wheelhouse where I now got to do my usual routine of being on anchor watch. The radios were tuned to the emergency channels, the radar was on and set on one quarter mile range to be checked every little bit, and the loran was calibrated to check our position and range of swing. While "sitting on the pick" in a storm such as that, the ship swung from side to side in a sixty-degree arc. The range of our swing had to be recorded and checked often to ensure we did not drag anchor.

The positions of the other ships at anchor were checked regularly while I made my hourly rounds through the entire ship while everybody else was sleeping. I would check the ship from top to bottom and stem to stern to make sure there were no fires or anything else wrong during the night.

At about 0700, the early light would start to make its appearance over the eastern, snow-capped mountains. The sky started to show a soft pink and yellow hue through the light clouds that now barely covered us. The storm had all but diminished into a light breeze and we had not dragged anchor, nor had any other ships.

As the captain made his way up the gangway and into the wheelhouse for the morning report, I had managed to guess right and had coffee ready for him when he arrived. I had to do most everything for the skipper to keep him in a good mood; from polishing all the brass in the wheelhouse to cleaning the head. Being the new guy on board had some advantages and disadvantages too.

After the rest of the crew had gotten around and we had somehow gotten an invite to tie up at the offloading dock, the Wookie and I made our way up to the anchor winch on the forward deck and hoisted the pick. Of course we had already picked a different crewman for the job of going down into the chain locker to coil the anchor chain as it came down the pipe. You can guess what happened to him too. Sometimes we just couldn't let any opportunity for mischief pass us by even if it didn't get the great results we had hoped for.

After we pulled up to the offloading dock and secured the mooring lines we finally could relax and leave the ship to go into town. Although the skipper and most of the crew left the ship, I headed for my bunk to get some well-earned sleep. There was always tomorrow.

Chapter 5

THE MAIL BUOY

When you're out in the middle of nowhere onboard a ship having to endure the loneliness of being away from home and working extremely long hours, two of the most treasured items are sleep and the mail. Sleep is the number one luxury item onboard a ship such as a processor. When the fish is piled up by the tons and you have the ability to process forty to fifty tons of fish per day, sleep will have to wait while the entire crew works to get them butchered, boxed and put away in the freezer hold. The storage hold on board the Denali could accommodate one and a half million pounds of product.

When working day after day for hours on end with only a break every few hours, one tends to get a little tired. The boredom that sets in even though you're working all the time is another factor that takes its toll. Since sleep is a luxury item and you want to get as much of it as possible, there is not much time left for too many other things. One of the little extra items that the crew looks forward to is receiving mail.

Getting mail onboard ship when you are miles and miles from

anywhere is a connection to the outside world. This connection serves a dual purpose: keeping your sanity intact and letting you know that there is life out there somewhere other than just onboard a big, black hulk of floating steel. Working on board a processing ship is like being in jail — with only the chance of drowning. You are confined to a two-hundred foot by seventy-foot area with only your shipmates to keep you company, and that can be an ugly picture sometimes.

Getting mail is one of the highlights that a person can really enjoy during their confinement. When time allows and you feel the need to write a letter to someone in the outside world detailing the grueling work that you do, the letter is deposited in the outgoing mail slot located in the galley. It was always a wonder as to when and how the mail got picked up and delivered to and from the ship. It was rumored that there was a secret mail submarine that came alongside just to pick up and deliver the mail and it was so secret that no one had ever seen it for sure. Another theory was that Bob, our cook, would somehow arrange for another ship that was headed back to port to pick the mail up from the mail buoy.

Bob's title was chief cook and bottle washer. With his very large body and the apron that he wore that was always black with grease, he was appropriately called the "Blacksmith." His culinary expertise was unmatched by anyone with a taste for the greasier side of food. It was a known fact that the food was considered gut filler. We were fed four times a day when we were working around-the-clock, which resulted in lines to the head for all those trying to eradicate the scourge that had rumbled through their gut. The menu consisted of several different items which ranged from cereal, coffee, eggs, coffee, toast, coffee, bacon, coffee, pancakes and coffee for breakfast, to sandwiches, coffee, hamburgers, coffee, spaghetti, coffee, fish and coffee for dinner. The snacks that were available during the fifteen-minute break period in between the regular meal times usually were coffee and cookies. Caffeine and sugar were staple items for the entire crew. It took just about anything and everything to keep us awake when working twenty or thirty hours at a time with only four or five hours of sleep in between work blocks.

The Blacksmith would be crammed into the little area that was the main grill and stove area with only a few inches of room on all sides of him. There was an assistant cook who performed a lot of the prep work but did not really do any of the grill work because there was no room for him to even get close to the grill when the Blacksmith was there. The Blacksmith was as happy as a clam at high tide there in the galley and he really liked what he did for the crew. He had an infectious smile and always had a big "hello" for all who wandered into his galley. When not pressed for time cooking one of the thousands of meals he put out for us, he would lumber out from behind the food counter and sit down at one of the tables to drink his coffee.

The man was a miracle worker with what he had for storage and the amount of equipment he had to work with. With a crew of forty-three people it was a constant challenge to keep up the pace he and the other cook had to face.

Several times during the six months on board the ship when we were sitting on the pick, some of the crew would be lined up around the railing casting a line into the water trying to catch fish. No matter where we were, there were always fish to be caught.

The little town of Sand Point, Alaska was a real nice place to catch fish even while moored to the fuel dock. All we had to do was throw a bare hook over into the water alongside the dock and we would catch codfish. There were so many of them there that they would jump out of the water to grab the hook if you dangled it just

47

above the water. I volunteered my expert cleaning services to the Blacksmith the day we were there, and we agreed upon fish and chips for dinner that night. Several of the crewmen and I caught five dozen codfish that day, and I filleted them and presented them to the Blacksmith for the final preparation. It was a feast loved by all, especially since it was fresh-caught that afternoon.

The Wookie and I of course were always looking for something to do when we were not up to our ears in work. We were well liked by the Blacksmith and he would occasionally back us up on one of our little schemes. The Blacksmith was a great bullshitter too. He could stand there and tell you a story and never crack a smile or let on to the fact that it wasn't the truth at all. You would swear it was the gospel truth if you didn't know any better yourself.

During any given week the outgoing mailbox would become pretty full, almost to the point that a grocery bag was needed to hold all of it. I myself contributed to it quite a bit, writing letters home about all the things that went on there on board the ship. The skipper would always ask me what the hell I found to write about, that there wasn't that much there going on for me to be putting out a book a week. I would just smile and say that there was all kinds of things going on, even him asking me so many times what I found to write about. He would just curse and shake his head and go off muttering to himself.

The Wookie and I conspired together to keep the skipper guessing all the time as to what we were up to so as not to foil our plans. The skipper would walk around talking to himself or, as was usually the case, curse us out for pulling something that he didn't particularly like. The Wookie and I would always come clean and tell him what we had done after the fact and I could tell that even though he acted a little mad, he was laughing inside at the crap we would pull off.

During the last week in Prince William Sound, as we continued processing the massive amounts of herring that were constantly coming to us from the fishermen, someone would notice that the mailbox was empty. They would ask when the mail went out, and when would the next batch of mail go out, because they didn't get their letter in the outgoing box. The standard answer to their inquiries was "soon."

Every answer to every question was "soon."

"When are we going to be done with all these fish?" "Soon," was the answer.

"When are we going to get to Dillingham?" one of the crew would ask. Again, the answer was, "Soon."

There was this young kid fresh out of high school that was trying his hand at sea duty to earn a little cash for college for the upcoming year. The owner had hired him out of the main office in Seattle. He was a good kid who was a hard worker and always ready to help out in any way he could. His name was Jim, a blonde haired skinny guy who had no idea what he had gotten himself into. Needless to say he was as green as new grass and had no clue as to the workings of a ship. He did whatever we told him to do, which was exactly what the Wookie liked.

The Wookie zeroed in on him like a barracuda after a tasty snack. On these particular occasions when the Wookie was on a roll, I usually just sat back and watched the fun as he delivered one of his long dissertations about one thing or another, telling the kid some wild tale that he didn't know whether to believe or not. Jim was frozen in awe at the details that were being presented to him; stories of the chain-locker beast, terrible storms that almost ripped the ship in half and the way our mail got picked up and delivered via the mail buoy.

At one point in the middle of all that bullshit that was being dumped on that poor naive kid, I surrendered my place at the table for a trip to the head since I had just eaten another one of the Blacksmith's fine meals.

Jim was told that the mail buoy was a special buoy that was used by several different ships that traveled the waters of the Pacific Ocean and the Bering Sea. The mail buoy was a very large, special yellow and black buoy with vertical stripes on the top of it and horizontal stripes on the bottom of it, with large arms that extended out from the sides. Each arm was several feet long with a hook on each end that was used to hang the ship's mailbag on. These buoys had a special radar reflector shield mounted on them so a ship's radar could see them, which let the passing ships know where they were. This, of course, was all bullshit.

As the Wookie was filling this kid's head with the mail buoy story, the Blacksmith wandered over to where they were sitting to listen in on this tall tale. Of course the Blacksmith knew what was going on and decided to help out a little bit by interjecting a few comments of his own. He told the kid that it was he who had to make all the arrangements for the pick up and delivery of the mail to the ship. The skipper would tell him when and where the next pick up would be and to get the mailbag out on the buoy for another ship to take our mail to port for us.

The Blacksmith told Jim it was a dangerous job that required good timing to hang the bag on the hook when it was rough out on the water. The lifeboat was a real challenge to stand up in for a guy of his size. When out in the lifeboat, I or the Wookie had to steer the boat and couldn't do both jobs so he had to be real quick as to reach the hook on the arm and hang the bag up.

While this little bit of information was being received by that greenhorn, I called the Wookie out of the galley to tell him that we were going to be setting sail in another day for Bristol Bay, and that we should delegate Jim as our lookout for the mail buoy. A huge smile came across the face of the Wookie and it became very apparent that he had already thought of the same thing. We had just the right man for the job.

The ship had received the last of the herring and was through processing it and getting them into the freezer hold to later offload onto a Japanese tramp ship. The Japanese were the main buyers of the herring and salmon we processed. Whenever we had to offload out on the open water it was usually to a Japanese cargo ship. After securing all the ships gear we hoisted the anchor and were under way again to another location for more work. We were leaving Prince William Sound and headed back to Kodiak to refuel, water and re-supply the ship with more provisions.

As the ship headed southwest toward the entrance and out onto the ocean, we again made our way through the large and small icebergs that filled the north end of Prince William Sound. Lucky for us this time it was daylight and the weather was good so, we did not need a bow watch for those Titanic-sinking chunks of blue and white ice cubes.

We were just about ready to stick our nose out into the ocean when we heard the weather forecast come over the radio calling for a big change out in the gulf. It was calling for storm warnings out in the Gulf of Alaska that day with seventy-knot winds expected. The skipper decided to anchor up in a cove just inside the entrance where we would be protected till the storm blew itself out and we could continue on across the gulf.

After a night of sitting on the pick in that calm cove we headed out into the open waters of the Pacific. The winds were still gusting to about twenty knots, but that was mild compared to what had come through the night before.

On the second day of traveling back to Kodiak, the Wookie and

I decided to put our plan to the test. We rounded up the Blacksmith and told him of our little plan to have Jim go on look out for the mail buoy. The Blacksmith was more than happy to assist us in our endeavor to embarrass someone. The Blacksmith waited until Jim came into the galley and then proceeded to cry his eyes out, telling Jim that the crew would be real disappointed if the mail didn't get delivered. When the Wookie and I met up with Jim in the galley, we informed him of the bad news.

"Our radar has blown a fuse and we can't get another fuse till we get to Kodiak," the Wookie said.

"We're going to need your sharp eyes out on the bow of the ship to look for the mail buoy so as we can get the mail out."

Jim was eager to assist us in looking for the mail buoy. We gave him a pair of binoculars and instructed him to stand up on the bow of the ship and let us know when he saw the buoy.

"You know what it looks like?" I asked him.

"Yeah I sure do," he replied.

I told him that it might be awhile so don't get discouraged, and that the captain was also looking for it from the wheelhouse.

He looked like a puppy dog with wide eyes and an eagerness to please his master as he went up to the bow of the ship to stand there and look for the mail buoy.

The Wookie and I wandered back up to the wheelhouse and upon entering we each grabbed a chair and sat there looking at the skipper. The skipper kept looking at us with a look of suspicion that told us he knew we were up to something again.

"What?" the Wookie said innocently as we looked at each other. But we could not hold back the chuckles of laughter.

The laughter then turned to hysterical outbursts as the skipper asked what the hell was that guy doing up on the bow of the ship with binoculars and what the hell was he looking for?

From the wheelhouse all the skipper could see was a guy dressed in a freezer suit standing on the bow of the ship intently looking all around the ocean with a pair of binoculars.

"Uh, he's looking for the mail buoy," I said still laughing.

"The what?" asked the skipper.

"The mail buoy." I repeated.

"Sure, you know, the mail buoy. That one we hang the mail bag on for other ships to pick up for us and take to port," the Wookie said.

As the laughter continued from all three of us the skipper kept calling us dirty, rotten bastards — along with a few other things that I care not to repeat.

Of course not wanting to be left out completely, the skipper grabbed the microphone to the loud hailer for the speaker up on the king post by the anchor winch and asked the kid if he saw the mail buoy yet.

"Not yet, sir!" he replied. "But I'll keep looking," he added.

The skipper turned and smiled at us as the Wookie and I almost fell to the floor laughing. I was surprised that the kid didn't hear us howling in the wheelhouse.

The Wookie and I left the wheelhouse and soon spread the word around to the rest of the crew about what had transpired and about our man on the bow of the ship looking for the mail buoy. Soon there was a dozen people up there on the bow of the ship asking him if he found the mail buoy yet. Jim had been standing up on the bow of the ship for several hours scanning the ocean waters intently for that elusive mail buoy.

A bolt of lightning must have hit Jim right between the blinkers because all of a sudden he stopped looking for the mail buoy and, with a look of total disgust, handed the binoculars to one of the other crew members and walked off to the bunkhouse on the upper deck without saying another word to anyone. The entire group of guys in attendance on the bow lost it and you could hear the roar of laughter go through the entire ship.

"I hope he isn't too mad," I said.

"He'll get over it," the Wookie said.

We never told anybody how we actually got the mail on and off the ship. The owner, who came and went quite often, was usually the one who would grab the mail bag whenever he left the ship and was headed for port but — nobody else knew that.

Chapter 6

ANIMAL HOUSE

The Denali was an old ship and like most other ships of her class that had been refitted for use as something other than what she was originally intended for, she lacked a few items that would be considered somewhat a practicality for the number of people that were on board. She carried a complement of forty-three people on her that included the captain, first mate and deckhands.

The cooks, engineers, and the grungy processing people made up the rest of the working crew. We all shared in the daily work of keeping that ship afloat and having to make do with what there was. The original structure and design of the ship only allowed for about half of what our total number was.

On the main deck of the ship there were six staterooms that housed the cooks, engineers and the Wookie's den. On the upper weather deck, in the main house, there were four more staterooms that housed the owner, bookkeeper, the captain's quarters and the first mate whom I was bunked with.

The captain's quarters were adjacent to the wheelhouse to enable him to respond to the bridge quickly if necessary. The first mate and I were situated in the second stateroom behind the captain's quarters so we could also be available also in case of an emergency where our presence was needed too. The staterooms were nothing short of a cracker box with a double bunk against the back wall and one desk. Our seabags were stored in a small open closet or under the bottom bunk. These rooms were mainly used for sleeping, and not much of that went on in them either.

One of the biggest deficiencies that this ship had was the lack of heads. A marine toilet is called the "head." On this ship there were only three heads. The main head was similar to a locker-room style setup with several showerheads and multiple stalls for the bulk of the male crew on board. This fine piece of work was located on the port side of the ship on the main weather deck adjacent to the processing house. On the starboard side of the ship there was another multi head that was just for the women that worked on board. They of course had their own setup since it was only right not to have to share with a bunch of animals. The third one was located on the upper deck next to my quarters. It was a unisex head used by the skipper, first mate, deckhands and some of the women too — although not at the same time.

I somehow was honored with the daily task of cleaning that head. How I came to receive that distinguished position is still a mystery to me. I guess being in the wrong place at the wrong time had something to do with it, plus the fact that I was the new guy got me that position automatically. Somehow the captain always knew if one of the processing crew had been in there. They would leave things not so clean after using the head and when the skipper would come out of there he would make it a point to let me know. Half the time he had me on "head watch" just to make sure that none of the "animals" would go in there and mess the place up.

If by some chance one of them did slip by me and used that

head without cleaning up afterwards, I would have to go in and clean it again. So I would have to play the heavy and tell the guys in the "animal house" that they would pay dearly if I ever caught one of them in there and worse yet if they left the head a mess. They would live to a ripe old age if they agreed to my terms and not desecrate the sanctity of the skipper's head.

The captain was one hell of a nice guy who appreciated a good crew, good work and a clean head. True, we were not military nor even remotely connected to such, but he was the captain and his decisions were the law on board that ship.

The skipper's name was Vaughn but he was also known by his nickname, "Captain Hook." He was nothing like the one-handed fairy -tale pirate in Peter Pan. He was somewhat of a pirate though in his own ranks, having spent many years sailing the waters around Alaska, and was a well-known commodity among the big boys of the commercial fishing industry.

His love of the sea and the life he lived was what made him the respected man he was. Though Vaughn never divulged very much about his past, occasional tidbits of information that did slip out revealed that he was once a scoundrel and operated on the shady side of things.

Vaughn was a short, round man with jet black hair, bushy eyebrows and glasses. He was a fast talker, great bullshitter and he called everybody "buddy." Everybody was his buddy, even the crew who he really would never get too close with because of the turnover. Processing people came and went like the tidal waters of Bristol Bay and he didn't have time to get to know them.

He pretty much kept to the immediate crew, meaning the ship's main crew that was there for the entire duration of the season. He somehow for some unknown reason took a liking to me and pitched me more shit than anyone else on board. The "Hook" would be totally mystified and always wondering how the Wookie and I wound up on board his ship together.

He thought it was bad enough with just one deckhand who pulled a bunch of shit all the time, but now he had two of us to contend with. The Wookie and I made it one of our priorities to always let the skipper know about most of the things we did so as not to leave him in suspense or cause him any undue hardships. Yeah right!

It was a battle of bullshit most of the time between us to see who was the most adept at doing almost anything that concerned the workings of the ship. From splicing lines to navigation we would provide each other with our undaunted ability to try and show one another up.

I was the king of knots and line splicing. I had the amazing ability to outdo everybody else in that particular endeavor and never passed up an opportunity to show off my expertise. Several of us would spend hours in the wheelhouse while the ship was under way showing off our ability to tie different kinds of knots and perform the many different splicing techniques.

Being a man who liked to take advantage of certain things, I would make bets with different unsuspecting fishermen who traveled with us to Bristol Bay for the herring season there, that I could tie a bowline knot in two seconds or less. The bet usually consisted of a case of beer or the money needed to buy one.

As a youngster I learned the fine art of how to tie what is called a flying bowline from an old salt that used this himself to win bets such as these. It was a simple maneuver that when perfected was a valuable tool to have stashed up one's sleeve for just such an occasion. After the bet was agreed upon, I would hold a piece of line in my hands and tell the guy to time me. As the words were falling from my lips I would perform the flying bowline in about one second and hold it up for him to inspect before he could even start timing me. A look of total amazement would be painted over his face and the words "do that again" would slowly roll out. Like a magician who just pulled off a masterful trick I would deny him the chance to see it again and collect my money. I loved making a little extra money from the people on board whether it was from card games or knot tying.

My greatest cache of wealth resided in the animal house. The animal house was an afterthought of the processing manager to house more people on board ship. The animal house was constructed at the beginning of the herring season and was a large, wooden box with ten bunks fastened to the walls. There were no tables, no water, and no sinks — just bunk beds for sleeping. The animal house was built on the aft portion of the upper weather deck behind the main house and between the two other modular sleeping units located on each side of the ship. Each of those modular units slept six people and were sparsely equipped with sinks and a couple of closets. They were almost one step up from the animal house. The animal house hung out over the sides of the upper deck and looked like it would blow off the stern in a bad storm.

The guys who occupied that house were of a different breed that rarely conformed to established protocol. They were a bunch of wild and crazy guys who didn't care one way or another to how much they drank when onshore at a bar, who they pissed off in those bars or much of anything else. They worked, ate, slept and generally just waited for their paychecks so as they could go do it all over again in the next port we got to spend a day or so in before we headed out to sea again.

The animals were somewhat ingenious as to scrounge up materials to make tables that they acquired from different places and brought back to the ship. The animal house was a fishy-smelling, stinky mess most of the time. All gear had to be stowed under the bottom bunks to keep it from flying around in rough weather so as not to knock someone through the wall.

The only stuff left out on the tables were cards, cigarette butts and porno magazines. This was a true bachelor pad of unmistakable quality. No woman in her right mind would walk within twenty feet of the door for fear of what might come crawling out of there.

Whenever I felt the urge to keep in touch with my insanity, I usually wandered into the animal house to see what I could accomplish in the way of lowering myself and increasing the money in my wallet. Those guys were game for just about anything that was presented to them if they thought they would have fun and possibly make some money too. To have a battle of wits with an unarmed opponent was truly a good thing.

When time allowed, I would walk in for a few hands of poker or cribbage and walk out a few dollars richer. They just never learned to say no to me when the opportunity arose for them to try and win some of their money back.

Once in awhile when the mood struck me just right, I would lower my standards and read to the guys the advertisements in the back of the porno magazines. I would make up my own commercials for the different types of sex toys and other strange oddities, which always resulted in incredibly raucous laughter from all the animals (keep in mind the mentality I was dealing with). It didn't take long for me to establish a following. They were always wanting me to make up more and more of my own commercials using all sorts of items in all kinds of odd ways.

Working thirty-plus hours straight was sheer hell, and this sort of thing was just what the crew needed. Any short escape, with bullshit thrown in by the ton, made it not seem so bad to be there.

Captain Hook never set foot inside the animal house. When he wanted to tell the crew something that concerned them, he would have the Wookie or me go in there and announce it. The skipper heard too many stories about that place and decided to avoid it like the plague. Nothing of any magnitude really ever did occur in there other than a couple of food fights and one of the animals getting too drunk one night and puking all over his bunk. That poor guy spent half a day cleaning that whole place up and fumigating it so the rest of his roommates could merely walk in there. That was probably the one and only time during the whole season that the animal house got cleaned.

It never ceased to amaze me the spirit that those guys showed when it came right down to the nitty gritty — when the work had to be done or a deadline had to be met. On many occasions I worked right alongside those animals and, on the flip side of the coin, it could be said that they were animals in the way they worked. They kept going and going. With the hours stacking up and the sheer exhaustion of working the processing line, those animals would hang in there and get the work done when it would have killed any ordinary guy.

The complaining would go on and on during this time but, as the old saying goes, a sailor is never happy unless he's complaining. If that holds true, then this was the happiest bunch of guys around.

Every now and then when things were just right and the mood was one of total exhaustion and stupidity, a fish fight would break out. If we were processing herring, those little fish would come flying through the air from out of nowhere. One by one, somebody would get nailed in the head by a flying fish that someone had thrown across the deck. Pretty soon there was a total work stoppage and everybody would be armed with herring and firing a volley at whomever got in their sights. This of course only happened when the processing foreman wasn't around. Once in a great while the foreman would catch the animals during one of their melees and all hell would break loose. The foreman would stomp around yelling and cursing at those guys to get back to work and generally threaten them with exiling them on a remote island in the Alaskan chain. The same thing occurred when they were processing salmon. It would start out with a little salmon heart, then slowly graduate to a complete gut pile being heaved across the room at someone.

One of the greatest accomplishments of the animal house crew was the diving contest. While at anchor in Ickatan Bay, which was located just outside of False Pass, during a break in the season between the time of herring and salmon, the animals decided to have a diving contest off the top of the animal house into the bay. Now as I said before, these guys weren't all there. The top of the animal house was approximately seventy feet off the water and death by some other means would be easier than jumping from there.

But they were not to be swayed off course from their goal of winning two cases of beer and a bottle of Jack Daniels, no, not by any measure. The judges were the Wookie and I, and we awarded the winner the undistinguished honor of craziest animal on board our fine ship.

To this day I still wonder how they ever came up with that stunt of trying to kill themselves for a couple of cases of beer and a bottle of Jack Daniels. Of course being that the Wookie and I were on the sidelines judging them, and it was the two of us that put up the prize, we suggested that a hint of madness would be in order just to see who was the craziest animal there.

The winning dive wasn't a dive at all so to say, it was a cannonball splash by a big man named Warren that won the prize. He walked away with the beer and the bottle and was not seen again for two days.

Chapter 7

THE
GREAT
HERRING
RESCUE

Quite often when working the abundant waters of Alaska, there are the times that things go right and there are the times that things go wrong. When things go right and all is well and you haven't a care in the world, it's a very nice feeling. It's a real joy to be out on the ocean when the weather is nice, the scenery is beautiful seeing the colors of the flowers on the faraway tundra during the summer months. The various ocean wildlife that is all around you never ceases to intrigue you as you watch walruses, seals, whales and birds go about their daily life in what can be a very harsh environment sometimes. In good weather, the salt air and the beautiful surroundings can make you never want to go back to civilization again. The sea and its alluring quality can take you and hold you in its grasp never wanting to let go.

The Sea

The sea is merciless
Mighty,
Cold.
Those who would love her
Must ever be bold.

She's lost many a battle,
But never a war.
Those who do woo her,
Are soon never more.

By first light She's peaceful,
Calm, quiet, serene
She promises wonders
No man's ever seen.

By morning She's playful,
A frisky young thing.
A portent for sailors
Take care or take wing.

The day's heat disquiets,
It shatters the charm.
Her faint hearted lover
Must flee or take harm.

The evening storm rages;
Waves batter the coast.
Her stout hearted lover

Will soon die —
Or boast.

Sun sets; Storm quiets
Her anger but foam,
The bone weary seaman
Reefs sail and goes home.

The sea is my mistress
My lover
My friend
My joy in her changes
I pray never ends.

The return trip to Kodiak once again was a well-earned break. We weren't able to spend much time at the Mecca on this trip since we were busy readying the ship for the "big one" in Bristol Bay. We had a nine-day westward voyage ahead of us along the Aleutian chain to Unimak Pass and our final destination of Togiak. We were scheduled to spend the next three months on the West Coast of Alaska without a break.

As the deck crew worked through the night, I was inspecting the main boom cable, and found a bad spot on the starboard cable. The main boom cable was a one-inch cable that ran the length of the boom arm and was loaded on the hydraulic drum reel at the top of the king post. This should have been the one thing that I should have never noticed because I then had to replace the cable. Replacing that cable meant I had to turn into a mountain climber.

On the sides of each seventy-foot high king post was a small steel ladder that had to be climbed to reach the winch. Once up at the top of one of these king posts, I had to unhook the existing cable and feed the new cable into the clamp down on the winch. Just getting to the top of the king post was a challenge in itself, let alone carrying another cable and my tools up to the top with me.

For some odd reason I could not pawn this job off on anyone else no matter how hard I tried. No bribe or promise could get me out of this job it seemed. I was stuck with it and everybody knew it too.

I managed to put my line handling experience to work knowing that I needed a harness to hold me to the ladder once I was at the top of the king post. Making a harness out of a cat's paw wasn't too hard and even attaching several short lines to me to hold all the tools and cable off my waist wasn't hard either, it was the weight of all that stuff climbing to the top of that little steel ladder that was the hardest part. Seventy feet of one-inch cable weighs a lot. Once at the top of the king post I proceeded to tie myself off to the ladder so as to have both hands free to work. It only took an hour to change the entire setup but I had an audience watching me with the expectations of seeing me drop to the deck like a sack of potatoes. As I untied myself and started back down the ladder, I saw and heard all that were watching me break out in applause for me doing the job that I couldn't pawn off on anyone else. I suspected that they all placed bets on whether I was going to splat on the deck or not but I fooled them by not falling.

The morning was cold and gray when we left Kodiak. Traveling through Shielakoff Straits, the wind was a steady twenty knots and the salt air in the early dawn hung like a semi-transparent blanket over the water being blown by the unseen force of nature.

For the upcoming season in Bristol Bay, the "company" had several fishermen and eight of their boats with us. Five of the boats were small enough for our ship's gear to lift them out of the water and lash them down on the main weather deck forward of the processing house. The three larger boats that traveled with us, we attached a towline to them and towed in tandem behind the ship.

The towline was the same line that was used as mooring lines for the ship. The line was nylon, three strand line that was three inches in diameter. Using two one-hundred-foot lengths of line, we attached a large truck tire in the middle between the two lines that was used as a rubber shock absorber.

So down the Aleutian chain we started, five boats on deck and three in tow. The ship was heavily laden with full tanks of fuel, water and fresh supplies in the storage locker. The added bonus of having three thirty-foot boats tied to our stern slowed us down too. Our breakneck speed of ten knots had now been reduced to eight knots. The ship's warp-core was being pushed to the limit.

It was during this time when the ship was under way night and day that the wheelhouse was the center of our universe. Most of the time you could always find several of the fishermen in there with us telling stories of their past adventures on the water, in bars and just about any subject they felt they could talk about.

I kept a small shovel standing in the corner of the wheelhouse with a list of names attached to it for special occasions when the bullshit got so deep we couldn't stand the smell anymore. When a story reached a particular point on the unsaid bullshit meter, I would grab that shovel and hand it to the guy who was telling the tale.

The difference between a fairy tale and a sea story is: a fairy tale starts with "Once upon a time" and a sea story starts with "This is no shit."

I wish I had a dime for every time I've heard the remark, "this is no shit." I could buy a few steak dinners with the money. Of course the time spent in the wheelhouse with some of those fishermen was fairly profitable for me also from time to time.

The voyage from Kodiak Island to Bristol Bay aboard a large, slow hulk is similar to the proverbial slow boat to China. Except for the engineers and the helm crew, there is not much to do during a nine-day voyage. To keep the rest of the crew entertained, there were several things that were done to ease the boredom for the restless crew. Card games were the most sought after form of entertainment. Cribbage tournaments, poker games and even an Uno tournament was held in the galley to help pass the time. While movies played on the galley television from the VCR, the shouts and cries from the players filled the galley like a Las Vegas casino.

The first mate came up with a challenge to anyone who wanted to try his or her construction abilities. He figured that since the ship was underway and we were on a nonstop voyage for nine days, he put up a challenge to anyone and have a kite building and flying contest. Any and all materials that could be found on board ship could be used. The best kite wound up to be a box kite made out of thin pieces of wood, duct tape and plastic garbage bags. The kite also had a long tail made from somebody's underwear. The kite string was a five thousand-foot roll of seine twine that was tied to the railing on the top of the processing house. That kite flew almost a mile away behind the ship. It would swoop from right to left like a pendulum, each time sinking lower and lower toward the water ready to splash down at any moment. But just when it looked like it would crash into the ocean, she would start climbing back up toward the sky. It would reach a certain height then start it's swinging motion again, falling back to the water. That kite flew like that for five days.

On the morning of the sixth day at 0600 when I was starting my shift, I had checked in with the first mate and the Wookie in the wheelhouse to get ready to take over the helm. After taking a position fix and plotting my course to steer for the next six hours, I left the wheelhouse to get the skipper and myself a pot of coffee from the galley.

In the galley a few of the crewmembers were still working hard at trying to drain one another's wallet in the ongoing poker game. The smell of grease, bacon, and coffee permeated the room as the Blacksmith was cleaning up the morning mess. It never ceased to amaze me how that man could put out the food he did. We never made rude remarks or got the Blacksmith mad. When you're trapped onboard a ship such as that one or any other one, whether it be in the Navy or merchant marine, the cook and the paymaster are the two people you never want to piss off or get mad at you. They need to be your best friends.

Having filled the two-quart thermos with fresh coffee for the skipper and I, I gazed out the aft windows of the galley sipping my first cup of hot, black mud.

In tow were the three boats bobbing along in our wake. As the first boat was lifted up and down over each swell, she began to dig lower into each swell. After three or four times of taking on a little water over her bow she dug under a swell and filled the entire cockpit with water. This particular boat was a bow-picker. With the cabin aft and the entire open cockpit forward, she dug into a steep swell like a shovel in soft sand taking on hundreds of gallons of water.

The huge truck tire that was tied in the middle of the towline as a shock absorber ripped in half from the weight of the waterlogged boat. The bow-picker drifted helplessly with her nose almost completely under water as she barely stayed afloat.

As I stood in the galley staring out over the stern witnessing this event, a feeling of numbness gripped me as my mind raced through the responses I should take. Of course a person is likely to do whatever they've been trained to do in an emergency, so the first thing I did was hit the panic button. The panic button is an alarm that, when hit, sets off bells ringing throughout the entire ship.

Everybody on board ship had been somewhat trained as to know what to do if that alarm was ever set off. At the onset of hearing that alarm, the group of guys that were in the galley performed what looked like a scene from an old Keystone Cops movie. Poker chips and cards went flying, bodies running into each other, and the attempted exit through the doors was not pretty either.

I quickly made my escape and made my way up the stairs to the wheelhouse and informed the skipper of what had just occurred. Captain Hook reduced the speed of the ship to one-quarter throttle and steered her hard to port. The Wookie and myself quickly un-hitched the lifeboat from the cradle and lowered it to the water. Taking three other crewmen and a few five-gallon buckets with us, we gave her full throttle and sped to the near-sinking fishing boat. As we fought through the waves to get to the sinking boat, we could see that big, steel hulk of a processor lumbering along making as sharp of a turn as she could to come about.

We had the three guys with the buckets climb aboard that boat and start bailing water out of her. In the meantime as all this was going on, the Wookie and I watched as the box kite that had flown for five days slowly descend into the ocean. We also watched as over five thousand feet of seine twine got wrapped around the cranes, the wires and the big king posts on the ship.

As the three crewmen continued to bail the water out of that bow-picker, the Wookie and I sped out to where the box kite had fallen into the drink. We had to save it too. After plucking the kite from the water, we motored back toward the floundering fishing boat. As the Denali drew closer to us and the three fishing boats, Captain Hook stepped out the door of the wheelhouse and promptly proceeded to yell at us and call us every name in the book with a few new ones added to the list. I then realized he had to have been the one who wrote that book. It seemed that the captain took a dim view of having almost a mile of seine twine wrapped around the rigging of his ship when she had to come about. The Wookie and I sat there in the lifeboat pondering our fate while watching the bow-picker slowly rise up to a level position again.

Having now saved one of our fishing boats from sinking and saving the kite, we used another large truck tire and reattached the towline to the boat again. After hoisting the lifeboat back into it's cradle, the Wookie and I commenced unraveling the twine from the rigging. With a sharp knife and a lot of climbing up and down the rigging, we finally removed all the twine. Captain Hook was still seething and continued to chew on us for a bit until I realized that he hadn't gotten his coffee yet. All this occurred before I could take the coffee up to him in the wheelhouse.

Without saying a word, I turned and ran out the door leaving the Wookie to face the remaining onslaught from the captain. I quickly ran to the galley and retrieved the thermos of coffee and returned to the wheelhouse. Captain Hook probably didn't miss a beat in his ass chewing but slowly subsided after I got him his coffee. I then came to the realization of how a person can come unglued before their first cup of coffee in the morning and resolved to hold off on all emergencies till the skipper has had his first cup of coffee in the morning. As I put the ship back on course and performed all the necessary navigational duties, I set the autopilot and sat back in my chair looking out over the blue-green water toward a distant point of land.

The next few days of sailing dragged by with not even so much as a joke or prank pulled off. We were getting restless and wanted to start working. There was just so much one could do while cooped up on a ship out on the ocean.

When we arrived at Nunavarshak Bay, it looked like a floating city of boats and ships. There were fishing boats, tenders, processors and big Japanese buying ships there all waiting for the season opener. The Alaska Fish and Game were out in full force with planes buzzing around overhead watching everybody so as to prevent someone from getting a head start on the season.

For everybody there it was the excitement and anticipation of a very good season. A lot of money was going to be made there all because of a little baitfish. Money is a big motivator. After nine days of no work for most of the crew, they were primed and ready to get with the program. The crew didn't have long to wait either because the season opened the very next day. By afternoon of that next day, we were up to our ears in herring; tons of them in fact. The work time usually lasted twenty-six hours at a stretch before we could take a break for sleep. The crew averaged five to six hours of sleep in between the long work segments.

At the end of the first week and thousands of pounds of fish later, we received a radio call from a ninety-foot tender who was coming to offload her fish on us. She asked us to be ready because she needed immediate attention—she was taking on water through her scuppers and was in danger of sinking. An hour later as I scanned the various boats that were in the area, I spotted her slowly coming toward us. She was the Man-O-War and was overflowing with herring.

She pulled alongside us and we tied her fast to us with our three-inch mooring lines. She had seventy tons of herring on her. Her hold was completely full and had thirty more tons on her deck. Her crew had used 2 x 12 boards to cover the scuppers so the herring wouldn't spill off the deck. The herring was piled in a mound seven feet deep on her deck from the aft main house to her bow. She was barely floating when she came alongside to offload. We worked for two days straight getting her unloaded and floating at her waterline again.

By this time I was starting to get pretty sick of the sight of those damn little fish, but we knew we still had a long way to go. We still had the rest of the west coast to cover before we would be even close to the end of this part of the season.

In between the long hours of work and the short hours of sleep, the Wookie and I usually found a litLle time to amuse ourselves with a little prank pulled here and there on some unsuspecting person. You'd think that most of the others would have caught on to us by then.

One morning while the Blacksmith was busily slinging slop... uh... er, making a fine breakfast for the crew, the Wookie and I decided to help out one of the processor crewmen. This young man wasn't quite ready for the enormous amount of herring we were receiving and was complaining bitterly about it.

The Wookie and I saw our opening and jumped on it like white on rice. We kept telling this guy that pretty soon he'll be seeing herring everywhere; that he'll even dream about them. So on this particular morning we asked the Blacksmith for a little help in preparing a special breakfast for him. Scrambled eggs, hash browns and herring sounded yummy to us. A separate frying pan was used and a nice fresh herring was diced up and added to his breakfast. The Blacksmith even used the tail for garnish on the plate. It added such a nice touch.

The Wookie and I sat there with straight faces and watched as this guy just stared at his plate of scrambled eggs, hash browns and herring.

"Hey! What the hell is this?" he bellowed.

"It's your breakfast," replied the Wookie. "What's the matter, you don't like seafood omelets?"

73

Well this little discussion went on for a little while to the chuckles and snickers of the rest of the crew that were in the galley. Our victim must have finally gotten the message when the Wookie finished chewing him out and telling him that we were tired of hearing his complaining. The Wookie and I sort of took it upon ourselves to be the morale officers of the ship. It was an easy job really because we just told whomever to shut their mouth (with an expletive thrown in here and there) and do their work. I know it wasn't very subtle but it worked most of the time.

As the season in one area would end and open in another one, the ship would travel north along the west coast of Alaska. Off the barren hills of tundra out in the icy waters of Norton Sound, walruses and seals lay on the surface of the water soaking up the sun's warmth as our ship lumbered along to its next and final stop at Unalakleet.

Unalakleet is a small Eskimo village several miles east of Nome and west of the Yukon River.

After we dropped anchor and had some time to ourselves, I went to grovel at the captain's feet to let me go ashore. I used every excuse I could think of to get off that ship and walk on solid ground. I even went ashore on a deserted island to walk around once just to be on solid ground. The main reason I wanted to go ashore was to find and use a phone. Every chance I got I would call home just to talk to my wife and kids. Besides, it was a lot cheaper to use a calling card than the marine operator. Staying in touch with the home world was the most important thing for me at that time. After going ashore I found that the village had one small hotel with a public phone. Ace scores again.

After I returned to the ship, I was right back to working on getting the processing line ready for this last area that we would be working in. This area was a restricted fishing area that only boats with gillnets could fish. Purse seiners fished most of the other areas. A purse seiner has a long net that is pulled off the fishing boat by a small skiff. While the skiff pulls the net off the boat and drags it in one direction, the fishing boat travels in the opposite direction and the two boats encircle the school of fish with the net. The net has a draw line at the bottom of it that closes the net when pulled tight. The net is then hauled back onto the fishing boat with a winch.

A gillnet is another type of net that is stretched out in a line or semi-circle. The mesh of the net is big enough to allow the fish's head to go through but not big enough to allow its body to make it through. When the fish swims into the mesh and cannot get all the way through it, the net catches it by the gill plates when it tries to back out or escape it. A gillnet is laid out like a trap for the unsuspecting fish to get caught in.

As our ship lay at anchor a short distance off shore, we rigged the five small boats on the main deck for lifting back into the water.

The fishermen that were working for the "company" could hardly contain themselves in anticipation of their season in these particularly abundant waters. The State Fisheries estimation of the amount of herring sounded very promising too. The small boats readied their gear and departed the mother ship venturing out to find just the right place in hopes of a large catch to start the season off right.

The Wookie and I made sure the line was ready to go again. We expected the fishing boats to start returning with fish at any time — and they did.

One by one the small boats would come alongside with their boats full of herring and sometimes they were so full they were dangerously close to sinking. As we worked hour after hour unloading the boats as quickly as possible, the crew continued to box and freeze thousands of pounds of herring. The crew gave up the chance for a few hours of sleep just so the boats could keep fishing and there was a chance for a longer break to be had after all the blast freezers were full.

Things had been working real good and moving along pretty smoothly the first week in Norton Sound. The boats were doing good and the crew was complaining as usual. "A sailor is never happy unless he's complaining" was the motto, so we must have had the happiest crew around.

We had about one more week to go before that area closed and we were all ready for it. But as luck would have it, everything started to go wrong — and all at once. The skipper received a call from one of our thirty-foot fishing boats. They had one of the small boats in tow and they were bringing her in to us. At first that didn't seem to be a real problem, at least not until they told us that the boat had sunk and was being held up by large boat bumpers. When the Wookie and I heard this we went out on the upper weather deck to see how far off they were and how bad the situation was.

Looking out over the starboard quarter we could see one of the larger fishing boats towing that small boat. There were two guys riding in waist deep water inside the boat. The boat had several bumper buoys tied to each side of it to keep it from sinking completely. They had their gillnet piled up inside the boat with the outboard motor laying on top of it. Under the gillnet the entire boat was full of herring. There was herring still caught in the net that they couldn't shake out into the boat because it was so full. The herring were spilling out everywhere as the two fishermen tried in vein to keep as much as they could in the boat, but they were fighting a losing battle.

Along with this frantic scene, there were hundreds of gulls and other water birds feasting on the overflow of dead herring that was pouring out of the boat and back into the water. Slowly they made their way over to our ship as we lowered the suction pump hose down to them. The two fishermen worked as fast as they could to get the rest of the herring out of the net while we pumped what was left of their catch on board and into a huge holding tank.

When the net got cleared and all the fish were unloaded, they bailed the rest of the water out, hooked up the outboard motor and came aboard to see how much fish they finally wound up with. They figured they had just over half of what they had in the beginning. When they pulled in their net, they could hardly believe the amount of herring that was in it. Filling the boat and having lots left still in the net, they got greedy and took it all on board their small boat. The weight was too much and they sunk their boat. If it wasn't for the other boats that saw them floundering, they might have all drowned.

Later after all was squared away and back to normal, the Wookie and I came to the conclusion that three near sinkings was enough fun and excitement for us for awhile. But Murphy's Law always seems to have a habit of jumping up and smacking you right between the blinkers and letting you know that if anything can go wrong — it will.

Captain Hook came stomping into the processing house and took the Wookie and I out to the foredeck.

"We have a big problem," he said with a hint of urgency in his voice. "I just got a report from the ships up north of us; they had to pull the plug and leave pretty fast."

Of course me being curious about that, I had to ask a very intelligent question, "How come?"

"The damn ice floe is coming this way and we have to get all the boats back here and get the hell out of here."

And so with a few choice words muttered by him about my intelligent question, he walked off toward the wheelhouse.

I had never experienced the ice floe but as I soon found out Captain Hook and the Denali unfortunately did the year before. Getting stuck in the middle of a continent of thick, almost solid ice and not being able to move other than wherever the ice floe takes you is a lonely and helpless feeling, not to mention the lost time and lost wages. For three weeks the year prior, the Denali and several other ships were trapped like bilge rats in a cage, waiting for an icebreaker to come and rescue them. The skipper did not want any part of that again this year.

The skipper managed to radio a couple of the fishing boats and told them to find all the other boats; that we were getting the ship out of that area as soon as possible.

After about an hour, the skipper came down into the processing house again and told the Wookie and I to pick the anchor. We left the processing house and walked out on the foredeck to the anchor winch. As we got situated and began bringing in the anchor I looked out over the port bow and could see the ice floe in the distance. It was moving slowly along at a snail's pace but fast enough to capture an inattentive ship and crew. As the anchor clanged its way up the side of the ship we saw that all of our boats were returning to our location. Like a mother hen and all her chicks, we made our way out of the path of that floating ice mass. When we had traveled far enough west back toward the Bering Sea, and there was no danger from the ice floe, we loaded the small boats back onto the deck and rigged the towline again for the larger boats.

With the herring season now at an end, we had but one more task to perform … and that was unload almost two million pounds of herring onto a Japanese tramp ship.

Chapter 8

TRAMPERS

In the world of high finance and big money, there are those who work at what they do very hard to get ahead in the business and there are those that don't. The big Japanese companies that invest in the business of buying fish on the high seas direct from the United States processors are as numerous as the mosquitoes in Alaska and sometimes just as pesky. Many of the Japanese companies each have several ships that are similar to a small freighter that sail the Pacific Ocean to the waters of Alaska to buy anything they can work a deal on. These ships are known as "Tramp Ships" because they travel from place to place making deals on herring, crab and salmon to take back to the main company in Japan. Tramp ships will have a crew of about twenty-six men, from the skipper who navigates her across the ocean down to the deck crewman. "Trampers," as we call them, and being who they are, is like dealing with a used car salesman. They may work for the "company" but out on the high seas it's a different ballgame. Trampers have their own company men that specialize in wheeling and dealing. It's simple really, they try to get the best price for whatever it is they're buying and we try to get the best price we can for selling.

The tramp ships are fairly large ships with three main cargo holds that can carry and keep the entire product frozen for the trip back across the ocean. They have large cranes on board similar to those aboard our ship that are used for transferring cargo. Some of the Trampers are in pretty good shape while others are nothing but rust buckets.

It's always a challenge to communicate with the crew on one of these ships due to the language barrier. However, there are times that the universal language of extending one's middle finger in their direction is understood when something gets screwed up during an important occurrence of coming alongside or the transfer of cargo.

When the deal is agreed upon between their company and our company, a time and place is arranged for the transfer. Sometimes depending on the area we're in and the company we're dealing with, the Tramper is already there waiting for us to start processing. The product goes directly from our big blast freezers to the tramp ship without us having to hold it.

When the time comes for us to tie up to a Tramper, the Wookie and I start gathering bets. Usually the bet is to see how many of the tramp ship's crew we can take out with the heaving lines when coming alongside to tie up. A heaving line is a small diameter line that is attached to the end of the heavy, three-inch mooring line. On one end of the heaving line, the throwing end, is what is called a "monkey's fist." A monkey's fist is a round pocket of woven line about two inches in diameter that holds a lead weight or links of chain to give it weight. The heaving line can be a hundred or more feet in length and is thrown from one ship to the other where the receiving ship's crew will pull the line in till they have the mooring line end. They will drop the mooring line end loop over a bollard, which is a large metal post. The loop end of the mooring line is called an "eye" which is spliced in the line. The mooring line is then pulled tighter on our side as the two ships draw closer to each other and then made fast as the ships come together. The other ship's crew unties the heaving line and tosses it back to us when all the lines are secure.

Sounds good in theory right? But you put a couple of guys like the Wookie and myself in charge of even the smallest task and we'll find some way of messing with it. Like the old saying goes, "If it ain't broke, mess with it till it is." This is not to say that we were incompetent, no, not by any means, we just liked to have as much fun as we could at whatever it was we were doing. This was just one of those things that we felt we could accomplish and not start World War III with the Japanese, although a foreign diplomat would probably call the state department and complain about us and our actions. We didn't try to kill anyone, only maim a few of them. When our ship would be approaching the Tramper, the Wookie and I were in charge of the lines. The Wookie would stand ready with the bow line ready to throw the first heaving line across. I was stationed amidships where I would throw the heaving line that was attached to the spring line. I would then run to the stern to make sure whoever was throwing that heaving line made it across so as not to wind up with a line wrapped in the prop. If that were to happen, whoever messed up throwing the line would have to go diving and unwrap it. And that water is colder than a brass bra on the shady side of an iceberg.

As the two ships drew close enough for us to toss the heaving lines across, the Wookie got the first shot. There were always multiple targets standing there on the deck of the Tramper waiting for the line to come sailing over to them.

With a quick swing of the monkey's fist over his head, the Wookie let her fly. The monkey's fist shot across the railing at those Japanese crewmen like a Nolan Ryan fastball. Those crewmen scattered like roaches running from the light. After that first shot was fired across their bow, I would follow suit with a missile of my own from amidships. I could usually make three or four of them hit the deck real fast with one powerful swing of the fist. After the incoming missile would shoot past them, we'd see their yellow hard hats pop back up from behind the side wall of the ship. Those Japanese crewmen would be yelling at us using words from the Japanese version of "the book," then would grab the heaving line and start pulling it in to get our mooring line across. After my spring line was across, I would run to the stern to make sure that the stern line made it across safely also.

One time when our ship was making its approach to a Tramper, one of the crewmen that was standing there with me got on his knees and begged me to let him throw the heaving line. He was so happy when I said "OK," I thought he was going to pee himself like a puppy dog does. I gave him the heaving line and a quick crash course on how to take out as many targets with one swing letting the monkey fist fly.

Well the eagerness and excitement were too much for him. When the time came to let fly with the heaving line, he swung the fist around and around over his head like he was a champion goat roper. Myself and one other crewman that was standing there had to hit the deck to avoid this cowboy's roping technique. He let that monkey fist fly almost as hard as he could throw it. It sailed through the air straight as an arrow; straight up to the conning tower damn near taking out the captain who was standing there watching.

Well that little misguided attempt almost caused an international incident. Captain Hook came out of the wheelhouse yelling at us, having witnessed that misplaced shot. Unfortunately I was the one who got chewed out even though I wasn't the one who made that impressive shot (almost wished I would have though).

Having the Wookie and I throw lead-filled monkey fists at those crewmen would normally be grounds for discipline, but things of this nature were usually dismissed rather quickly and the two ships and their crew would soon be engaged in international trade.

We would trade Playboy and Penthouse magazines for Saki and whiskey and just about anything else that favored good international relations.

After securing all lines and our initial friendly greetings were over with, we would start getting everything ready for the offloading process. Each ship would lower their inside boom arms down and hook the outside boom arm cables together. Each ship with their hatches removed would have a crew in the hold to fill and empty the cargo nets. Our crew in the hold would fill a cargo net then hook it up to the crane. I would then lift the full net up two decks till it cleared the railing. As I did this, the crane operator on the Tramper would haul in on his cable while I would slack off on mine. They would then lower the full cargo net down into their hold, unhook it and hook on an empty net for me to bring back across.

In the meantime, our crew would be loading another cargo net full of frozen, boxed fish ready for hook up and transfer to the Tramper. This offloading of product would take a few days to accomplish working two crews six hours on and six hours off.

Of course no day would be complete without the Wookie and I pulling off some kind of stunt. On the last day of offloading cargo, the Wookie and I thought it would be fun to let one of our crew experience Japan from inside the hold on their ship. The Wookie and I had randomly selected a candidate to enjoy this bit of cultural diversity. The Wookie and I thought about the implications of this particular plan a lot before we decided to do it. I think we thought about it for two seconds maybe.

We were going to be a little daring with this plan, as you see, we chose one of the eight female crew for this little stunt. The Wookie and I informed her a few times about how these Japanese sailors liked young, American women. We told her that she would be safer on board our ship and not to go aboard their ship or she would get a free trip to Japan.

She was a girl that was going to college and earning money during the summer months on board our ship. A lot of the processing ships in Alaska had women working on them and we were no different.

As the third day of offloading almost two million pounds of herring came upon us, the Wookie and I, along with the help of the other freezer rats that worked in the hold stacking boxes in the cargo nets, felt the time was right for a little excitement. However, all the excitement was going to be for this one particular lady.

I was standing on the main weather deck operating the crane as the freezer rats stacked two layers of boxes on the cargo net. I could look down and see that the boxes were not positioned right on the net so I yelled down to our female crew person who was standing there to climb on there and get them all straight. As she did this, four guys quickly picked up each corner of the cargo net and threw the loops on the big chain hook trapping her inside the net.

I quickly lifted the net with her inside it as she screamed a few choice words at us. At first she just yelled and cursed at all of us but soon her voice changed into one long wailing scream. As the net cleared the main deck hatch, I stopped the crane and hollered at her before she started traveling across to the Tramper.

"Hey! We sold you for ten cases of Saki and Scotch," I said.

At this point the wailing and screaming stopped for a few moments. She just sat there looking as frozen as the boxes of herring she was sitting on. She had this very quizzical look on her face that soon turned to a red, angry-looking one. If looks could kill, the Wookie and I would have been dead in a heartbeat.

She then erupted again like Mt. St. Helens, screaming at us after I told her that I hoped she liked Japan and eating raw fish.

The crane operator on the Tramper took her and the cargo net half full of herring across like any other load while she continued to scream and curse at us. As she was lowered into the hold and disappeared out of sight, the Wookie and I stood there waving goodbye to her as we could still hear her voice echoing from the hold of the tramp ship.

After a short pause, the crane operator of the tramp ship lifted an empty cargo net up and I in turn hauled it across to our ship and lowered it into our hold.

It took several minutes, but appearing at the top of a ladder coming out of the Tramper's hold came our crew person. This time she wasn't yelling and screaming when she walked across the gang-planks back aboard our ship. In fact she was smiling a little. It was sort of that smile you see when somebody has a secret about something good.

Without saying a word, she walked into the main house and went back down into the hold and started working again. This sort of thing left us all scratching our heads and wondering what she was up to.

We finished up the offloading that evening and secured all hatches and booms. The captain from the Tramp ship and our own captain had spent most of the evening having dinner and visiting aboard the Tramper before we were to set sail back to Dillingham in Bristol Bay. As the crew from each ship waved their good-byes, one of the crewmen from the Tramper walked over the gangplank carrying a big box .The female crew person that took the ride over in the cargo net met him there and was given that big box he was carrying. She in turn handed him a bag and he bowed to her before he turned and headed back aboard his ship.

The Wookie and I stood there watching this as she took the box and walked down the walkway to her quarters. The Wookie and I stared at each other with the look of, "I don't know what that was?" as we readied the lines for retrieval.

The gangplanks were pulled aboard and the mooring lines were hauled in and flaked over the railing. As the Denali shuddered and shook with the engine in reverse, we were on our way again. As soon as we were squared away, the Wookie and I, just out of curiosity, went to the females' quarters. After knocking on their door, we were met by our traveling cargo net lady who politely said, "Yes, can I help you?"

The Wookie, not being one to beat around the bush, asked her what was in that box she got from that guy on the Tramper. Without batting an eyelash, she nonchalantly said, "Oh, just a case of Scotch."

Well that's all it took for the Wookie to start drooling and almost come unglued. He wanted to know what she traded for it and how she got a whole case of Scotch?

"Well it's really none of your business," she said.

After a few more attempts of trying to get her to divulge information and not succeeding in getting any, we left her quarters and walked up the stairway to the wheelhouse.

"I can't believe it!" the Wookie exclaimed as we entered the wheelhouse. "She got a whole case of Scotch!".

Captain Hook sat there in his chair with a smug look on his face thoroughly enjoying this event. Seeing the Wookie totally distraught having been outdone by a crew person was sheer pleasure for the Captain.

When the Wookie left the wheelhouse to go get some coffee in the galley for us, the skipper told me that the case of Scotch was his and that he wanted to play a little joke on the Wookie. You see, the captain was over on board the Tramper in the hold with the tramp ship's captain when our lady friend took her little voyage in the net.

Captain Hook thought this would be an excellent opportunity to give the Wookie a little dose of his own medicine. Since the skipper was already getting the Scotch, (part of another deal made earlier) he had the female crew person take the delivery of it and tell us it was hers.

Scotch was the Wookie's favorite beverage to indulge in. I myself can't stand Scotch or Whiskey— makes me sick just drinking one ounce of the stuff so I didn't really care about the whole deal.

So for the entire three-day journey south to Dillingham, the Wookie was constantly reminded of that case of Scotch that the crew person received. Whenever the skipper got the chance to rub a little salt in that wound, he always did a good job at it.

It was such a good dose of his own medicine that the skipper gave the Wookie, it lasted the rest of the salmon season. The Wookie was finally told what the skipper did to him at the end of that season.

"What can I say?" the Wookie exclaimed, "He got me."

Chapter *9*

ICKY BAY
PARTY

It was a long, slow trip for all of us that had just spent several weeks getting no sleep, rescuing sinking boats, and the usual work of processing almost two million pounds of herring. We had hoped that somewhere along the way we would get a break from all the fun we were having. I almost got to the point of masochism, not knowing the difference between pain and real pleasure. We soon found out that the herring season was just a warm-up for what was to come in the not-so-distant future. The salmon season was not quite ready to start yet but we had already started tearing down the herring processing line and were making plans for those other slimy fish to come aboard.

We had hooked up the boats again behind our ship and had put those five smaller boats on the main deck to transport them back to Dillingham where they were going to be stored for the rest of the season. I had spent the prior summer in Dillingham and I felt like I was going to revisit a nightmare in Bristol Bay. We also had a change of several crew people that left the ship when we got to Dillingham. I guess they couldn't stand the Blacksmith's cooking and just had to desert the ship for more exquisite cuisine. I had thought about it too for a brief time being that I was losing more weight than I cared to. I wondered if I could get another type of meal there in Dillingham other than caffeine, grease and sugar.

Of course those are three of the four main food groups, with alcohol being the only one left out. I knew I could get that fourth one if I could abandon ship and make it into Dillingham for one night. I still knew a couple of pirates there that could provide me a splendid time for a night with some fine company. But as luck would have it, the ship didn't stop in port nor did it stay long enough for any of us to go ashore and enjoy that fourth food group. We usually had our own supply with us on board but the "Hook" forbade the indulgence of spirits on board while we were working. It almost made some of the crew lean a little bit to the mean side of their attitudes not being able to partake of a needed adjustment.

Even I regressed to a point where some people would say that I had an attitude problem. I would tell them that they were gravely mistaken, that I didn't have an attitude problem, they had a perception problem and I would be more than happy to assist them and have them swim back to shore from out in the middle of Bristol Bay if they wanted to. I was always a happy and caring guy ready to assist anyone with any problem that they might encounter. After all, being one of the guys who helped keep the morale up was sometimes very time-consuming.

The future agenda looked a little foggy as to where our next port of call would be. The supplies were starting to get low; the water maker had been working overtime at peak capacity to keep up with the demand for fresh water and the huge fuel tanks were starting to get dangerously low. In fact, the ship was so light that she would rock almost twenty degrees more to either side when in choppier seas. That was a lot for a large ship such as that and it sort of made the skipper a little uneasy.

The entire crew had been put on water rationing and had to conserve water for several more days before we could fill the tanks that held thirty thousand gallons. We were under orders to take what is called "ship showers."

A ship shower is really a rather simple task. This is where you get into the shower, turn the water on and, trying to stay out of the way of the ice water that comes out of the showerhead at first, you quickly get your head and body wet. This is of course you can stand glacier water tempetures on your already cold body.

After you've stopped jumping around from the shock of having stood under cold water, you turn the water off — now making it even colder than when you first got in the shower. No fair letting the water run until it gets hot, that is considered wasting water. Then as fast as your frozen limbs can work, you quickly soap down your entire body using what little water is still left on your skin. After scrubbing your hair, face, and body with that ratio of soap to water, you are now coated with a thick paste of soap. At least this is the best part though — you get to turn the water back on and wash that crap off of you now. By this time the water has had a chance to warm up a little more and you are no longer an ice cube in there anymore. As soon as you have rinsed off, you immediately shut the water off again, hence saving many gallons of water. It was good enough to get the slime off you but not much more.

As the ship continued its slow pace through the Bering Sea, the captain was wondering about where we were going to refuel, water and supply. The closest place to us was Dutch Harbor. In Dutch Harbor, we could just about get everything the ship needed plus a few other things the crew needed too. Since we were scheduled to hang around this neck of the woods it seemed like the most appropriate place to dock.

The crew was pretty well spent by now and the days slowly melted one into another. Just the few days needed to travel seemed even longer with the long daylight hours of summer coming upon us. During this time of year out on the Bering Sea we could watch the sun as it would fall toward the water. The sun would slowly descend on the horizon filling the sky with a multitude of colors. Reds, yellows and oranges glowed like fire against a steel blue backdrop of a sky. The sun would dip down to the water's darkness threatening to extinguish its blazing orange colors, but the sun refused to disappear below the water.

As though time stood still for a brief moment, the colors that filled the entire sky seemed to freeze in a perfect mixture. The perfect blend of subtle colors would then slowly start to change again. What was soft, intertwined colors now began to brighten with the sunrise. The reds, yellows and oranges begin to glow more brightly as the sun would start its long climb back into the sky.

Soon all the distinguishable colors would fade into the bright white of the morning light, as the sun would take its place again high above the water. The light of dusk is as dark as it ever got during that time of year.

As the ship was approaching Unimak Pass, the skipper received a call on the side band radio from Alaska's premier lady of the airwave, Peggy. Peggy was the voice of Alaska for the entire fishing fleet. She announced the weather reports for all to hear and was the relay person for important messages too. Every captain on every ship out on the water loved and trusted her because she was a major communications lifeline for just about everyone.

Peggy hailed us just when we were about to change course and head for Dutch Harbor at Unimak Pass. She informed us that our company owner had made arrangements for us to dock at Sand Point. Sand Point, Alaska is located in the Shumagan Islands about halfway back up the chain toward Kodiak Island. This little detour now would tack on an additional day or so of travel time. We were not very happy to say the least, but we were able to bring her hard to port and make our way through the pass without having to back-track.

It took us all morning and most of the day to get to Sand Point. When we arrived we found a nice long dock open and waiting for us. As we tied her fast and shut down the main engine, the supply steward who would see to our needs met us. He worked closely with our engineers and cooks to make sure we got everything we needed.

That afternoon some of the crew and I discovered how good the fishing was right there alongside the boat. As I previously stated, the pacific true cod were so numerous and so hungry, that we caught them one after another with just a bare hook dropped into the water. That evening after the entire crew stuffed themselves on fish and chips, the captain gave the go-ahead for all to go ashore and enjoy themselves.

Since we had most of our work done it was a welcomed break to get off that ship and destroy a few million brain cells. We found the one and only bar in town and proceeded to relax in style. Playing pool was a real challenge because the pool tables were just slightly off center; sort of like playing on the roof of an A-frame house. The beer wasn't very cold but most of us didn't care just so long as we could relax for an evening.

At about two in the morning, a couple of new guys who hired on at Dillingham got pretty tanked up and got into a fight outside the bar, then wandered off to who knows where to empty out the contents of their stomachs.

The captain and the rest of us headed back to the ship and made ready to leave later that morning after an aspirin martini to silence the jackhammers in our heads. The Wookie and I hauled the lines in and the ship departed Sand Point with new orders and two less crewmen.

The two guys that were drunk and got into a fight missed the boat. I'm sure they finally woke up somewhere on that island and realized they didn't have a job anymore when they got to the dock and saw that the ship was gone.

With new orders in hand, our ship and company were sailing west again. For this year, three processing ships were leased by one U.S. company to sell salmon to one large Japanese company. The three ships, the Nicole N, the Clipperton and the Denali were to meet together at False Pass, Alaska before the salmon season began.

As we were making way along the coastline, we received a radio call from the other two ships. They said they were only a short distance away from False Pass and would be anchored in Ickatan Bay just outside of False Pass.

When we arrived at Ickatan Bay, the other two processing ships were already anchored up. The Wookie and I dropped our anchor and made ready the lifeboat to take the captain and the first mate into False Pass so as they could meet with the other two skippers and the big company man in charge of this upcoming event.

As the ship's lifeboat man, I was privileged to hang around and attend the meeting of the minds concerning this planned attack. The business at hand was a rundown of what each ship could and had to do, what their capacity was and where they would be headed during the season. Each ship had it's own unique capability when it came to how fast they could process the fish and how much they could hold till it was time to offload onto a Tramper.

As the mathematics were worked out and the different options decided upon, that big company man came up with a great idea to start the season off right. He strongly suggested that the three ships get together and have a party on Ickatan Island. What he really wanted was to have everybody get the urge to drink and party out of their system before the season started so there would be no mess-ups when it was time to work.

As we ventured back out to our ship, Captain I look told me to put the good news up on the message board in the galley for all to see. As we pulled alongside our ship there were three crewmen that had brought out their fishing rods and were already fishing off the stern of the ship. The skipper and first mate started to climb the ladder on the stern when, just before they reached the deck, one of the crewmen hollered out that he had a big fish on. He started running along the railing with his fishing rod in hand not looking where his line was and proceeded to almost decapitate the skipper who was still on the ladder.

I sat in the lifeboat watching the captain flail his arm around trying to remove that fishing line from around his neck. But even more important to me was the fact that that crewman did indeed have a big fish on. I turned all my attention to the guy with the fish on instead of worrying about whether the skipper was going to fall into the drink or not. I positioned myself alongside the ship where I thought the fish would make its appearance and I could gaff it and bring it in to the boat.

This battle went on for quite awhile with that brut our crewman had on the end of his line. Gaining line then losing it again seemed to be the norm. Just about the time he thought he could get that fish up to me in the boat, that carnivorous creature would dive back to the bottom again. After forty-five minutes of wearing this beast out, we got our first look at it. It was a halibut of immense size. It looked as big as a barn door in the water and I knew I was not going to be bringing that fish into the boat with me using a little gaff hook. I estimated that flat fish to weigh over a hundred pounds and didn't really feel like wrestling around with it in a sixteen-foot boat.

I yelled at one of the other crewmen that was standing there watching us to run and get the Wookie and his gun; that we were going to have to shoot this fish to kill it. So off he ran to get the heavy artillery so we could have a feast with this fine catch.

Having been a sport and commercial fisherman for many years, I knew how to handle one of these behemoths. I told the guy who had this fish on to just let it hang under the surface about ten feet down and not to put any pressure on it. That big slab was tired and didn't have much fight left in her.

The Wookie showed up with his .22 cal rifle, climbed down the ladder and got into the boat with me. I slowly pulled that big halibut up to the boat and told the Wookie to pump a few slugs in its head just behind the eyes. He shot it three times real fast as it broke water next to the boat and hit it in the perfect spot because that big fish just quivered on the surface of the water. I stuck the gaff hook through its mouth to hold it alongside the lifeboat. I then took a long piece of line and fed it through its mouth and out the gills. I tied a knot in the line and threw the other end up to the guys on deck.

I yelled at them to haul away and pull her up the side onto the deck. They hoisted that hundred-plus pound halibut right up and onto the deck with no sweat. Amazing what a little adrenaline can do for you with a prize catch like that even after fighting that fish for forty-five minutes. By now there was a crowd gathered around to see this big fish get brought on board. The crew could hardly believe that there was a fish that big in only forty feet of water where we were anchored.

I secured the lifeboat and went into the galley to write the good news about the party on the main message board. After I wrote the orders on the board, I walked out on deck where quite a few people were still gawking at that big fish. With several pictures taken of the big catch, the guy who caught the fish didn't really know what he was going to do with it.

I made the suggestion that the big halibut could get cooked up for the party. Everybody stopped talking and stood there looking at me in total dismay. They had not yet seen the message board and couldn't quite comprehend what I had just said to them.

"Party? What party?" someone asked. I told them what had transpired earlier and that we had a few days to party before the salmon season got going. I told them the company that is leasing our ship and the other two processing ships wanted to have a big party on Ickatan Island to get "it" out of our system before the season started. As close as I could figure, those crewmen scattered like wildfire to go inform the rest of the crew in the animal house of this upcoming event.

I got the go-ahead to fillet the halibut and give it to the cooks to prepare for the party for the next day. The cooks worked half the night preparing food for the big party. Not only did our ship make lots of food, the other two ships also contributed to the cause. We estimated that there was one hundred and fifty people who were going to invade Ickatan Island at around 0700.

Ickatan Island was a small, uninhabited island that afforded easy landing access on the beach. From the beach inland for about sixty yards was a grassy, flat field on which we sat up the makeshift tables for the food. The tables were made out of old pallets and driftwood which worked fine until some people got a little too drunk and fell on them.

On the island just on the other side of the grassy field was a small lake. The lake was the size of a football field that stretched to the sloping hills behind it on the island. That lake was a major source of entertainment for a lot of people who liked to go swimming although they didn't wear swimsuits.

With the morning hours drawing near, most of our crew were awake and ready to go get started with the easy task of trying to damage their liver and kill millions of brain cells. When all the food, beer and whatever else was ready and slated to go ashore, I loaded as many people as I could into the lifeboat carrying all they could handle and took them to the beach to this huge event. All three ships had a continuous stream of people going ashore carrying food, booze and anything else they might need for their survival on an uninhabited island for a few days.

Several hours into the first day of getting acquainted with the other ship's crew, the Denali crew challenged the other two ships to a game of football during the festivities. It was a friendly game of tackle football with no pads, and it really didn't bother us to get hurt after several hours of drinking. Everybody was numb from the alcohol so it really didn't hurt too much to get stomped into the ground. At least it didn't hurt me or some of our team due to the fact that we had the biggest guys there and that one of our guys was a running back for the University of Washington Husky football team. We had a ringer that the other teams didn't know about. Needless to say it was a slightly unfair advantage for us, but one we didn't mind especially when it came time to collect the winnings from our bets.

That evening when most everybody got into his or her comfort zone, the debauchery started to overflow. People became less and less inhibited as the overeating and alcohol took hold of them. While music blared from a boom box, a few ladies started doing a strip tease for the audience. That got a loud uproar from the crowd of onlookers and some of the guys there started putting money in the girls' underwear. A few couples snuck off into the hills for their own private parties not wanting to be seen by others and, of course, the ever popular wet T-shirt contest was a big hit for all the guys.

The next day when most of the people woke up after having passed out from obliterating millions of brain cells, they picked up almost right where they left off. With the weather being as nice as it could be in Alaska in June, several people went for a swim in the lake to wake up and clear out the dead gray matter in their head so as to make room for more casualties.

As the party continued into the next day, it became apparent that the supplies of food and booze allotted for this occasion were running dangerously low now that the revelers had won the invasion of Ickatan Island. The crowd of people was dwindling fast with each launch boat taking more and more crewmembers back to their ships.

The Wookie and I during this festive event had staged the diving contest from off the top of the animal house as part of the craziness that all were part of. Several people from the other ships looked on as each person who participated gave it their best shot of trying to kill themselves with a leap into the cold waters of Ickatan Bay.

I had pretty much wore myself out from the previous day and night's activities and was ready for a little rest. It's amazing how much energy a person can expend at a party trying to relax and have a good time. So the only way I could get away from all the hard work and self-abuse of killing brain cells was to go hide and try to sleep.

Trying to find a place to sleep and not be disturbed aboard that ship was like trying to sleep in the middle of Bourbon Street during Mardi Gras. I couldn't go to sleep in my bunk because there would be a steady stream of interruptions of people knocking on my door wanting me to operate a crane or something. I came up with a solution to my dilemma of trying to find a hiding place by rigging a hammock in the upper reaches of the fidley. The fidley was the perfect place to sleep. The continuous, steady sound of the generators humming away and the nice warm area among the pipes was just the ticket. Not many people came and went through the hatchways below so I could pretty well disappear and not be found.

I did however tell the skipper where I was so that I could be yarded out of there if needed.

The rest of that day and all night was just a blur of lost time in the one luxury item that we so seldom ever got. I slept for twelve hours straight before I was awakened and told that we were going to start getting the line ready for the salmon opener there at False Pass.

Everybody had had their fun and received the chance to drink him or herself into a complete stupor, but now it was time to get ready to go back to work and appreciate the good time we had had.

Having been up in that hammock caused quite a stir among some of the crew. Seems that some people were looking for me and thought I had jumped ship or had wound up as a bear's dinner since I was nowhere to be found. Too bad for them that I showed back up because the Wookie and I still had plans for the rest of the crew. This was one of our main goals in life aboard the Denali, to try and have the most fun we could despite the long hours of work that we had to do.

Soon everybody was barely alive again and almost ready to get with the program. Most of the crew was a little slow to get moving since it took some time to recuperate from the three days of self-abuse and trying to have too much fun.

Chapter *10*

THE SLIME
LINE

Usually the start of the salmon season is a little on the slow
side. The peak of the season comes later on after a week or two of
fishing. The salmon start to get that urge and begin to gather in
bigger schools and feed heavily before starting their journey up
the rivers to spawn.

Years ago when I was in Ketchikan, there was a street at the
north end of town that the fishermen would crawl up to go spawn.
That was after some fool of an old salty dog would try to complete
the "circuit." The circuit was the first two streets along the water-
front that were lined with bars one right next to the other. It was a
standing challenge for a sailor to try and make a complete trip up
and down both sides of the street and drink one beer in each bar.
I don't know if it was ever done or not, but I for one was a light-
weight and didn't even make it to the end of the first block. I knew
then I could not make it as a heavyweight in the drinking business.

Our ship and crew with its luck seemed that we were destined
for a brutal season of long hours and lots of fish. The company had

spent quite a few dollars on increasing our productivity with the purchase of new machinery.

Usually all things considered, when theory is put into practice, there are a few bugs to get worked out before things go as planned. The optimum performance of any given work is directly proportionate to the human ability to screw it up. So when we were told that the new machinery would make it possible for all of us on the butcher line to be able to process thirty fish per minute, we would see to it that it was feasible. Yeah right.

When working, most all of the crew was paid by the hour. So it seemed to them that the longer they worked, the more money they made. It was very common to be working along at a steady pace and then have someone yell out "Milk break!"

Everybody in the processing house would stop working and proceed to stand there moving their hands up and down as if they were milking a cow for a few minutes. It was called milking the clock and the slime line was the best at it when it came to grabbing a few extra dollars. What would normally take eighteen hours at a stretch could be drawn out to twenty hours without the blatant, outward appearance of them really doing it on purpose. This was accomplished when the processing foreman was not standing around breathing down everyone's neck. He was the man that yelled and hollered at everyone to keep going as fast as they could go. Of course him being a company man and being salaried, he was the designated whip to try and hold down the cost that the company paid out. Everybody liked him because whenever he would start to leave the processing house, some salmon guts would be thrown at him to let him know that we truly adored him. Once in awhile he would walk backwards just to try and spoil someone's pitching practice.

The butcher or "slime line" as it was called was art in motion and resembled a fingerpainting done by a pre-schooler. Although it did have it's bright moments now and then when we could butcher sixty-five hundred pounds of salmon an hour, it was still a challenge to measure up to the expectations of the company. The slime line consisted of twelve people that all worked together to accomplish the goal of taking a whole salmon, cutting the head off on what was called a "header," cutting the stomach membrane, completely cutting and gutting the fish as they were put through a "Ryan machine," and cleaning out any leftovers before the fish was quality graded and sorted.

As soon as one of the big fish totes got full, it was taken out of the processing house onto the main deck and sent down the elevator for further processing. Between decks another crew would be at work laying the salmon in special four-foot-by-four-foot shallow, wire baskets that had a nylon liner in the bottom so the salmon wouldn't freeze to the basket. Each basket held ten or twelve salmon and was stacked one upon another on a pallet. We would stack them eleven baskets high then place up to twenty-two pallets in each of four blast freezers. The salmon would be frozen to a minus ten degrees in about twenty-six hours.

With all four blast freezers full, it was somewhere around sixty thousand pounds of salmon we were able to freeze every time we filled all the freezers. This was only the first part of the line to be accomplished before the final product was ready for transfer to a Japanese tramp ship.

As our ship would be unloading a tender full of salmon using a fluid fish pump where the pump sucked the chilled water and fish out of the tender's hold, the fish would travel through a ten-inch diameter hose into the large pump. The fluid fish pump was like a very large Shop Vac, but with the ability to pump all the water and fish out of it too. So we could fill her up and empty her in just a few minutes.

The fish, upon being expelled from the pump, would travel through another ten-inch diameter hose from the main deck up onto the roof of the processing house. We had cut a hole in the roof and built a plastic nylon shoot for the salmon to go through and drop into a large hopper inside the processing house. The hopper held approximately five to six thousand pounds of salmon when full. On one side of the large hopper was a door that emptied out into another smaller hopper. That was where the slime line began.

The salmon were taken out of the small hopper and placed on the table that had the header. The header, or "iron chink" as we affectionately called it, was an air-compression guillotine that could chop the head off a fifty-pound Chinook salmon in a split second. I operated the iron chink most of the time and can say that I still have all ten of my fingers left. Unlike what happened to a crewman aboard another ship that lost one of his fingers to the "Iron Chink" because he wasn't paying attention when putting salmon into it.

After lopping the head off a salmon, the head falls through a hole in the table and into a hydraulic grinder that grinds up all the heads and guts, not to mention fingers too. The whole mess was then washed out an eight-inch diameter hose that extended back beyond the ship in the water. You could always tell when a processor was working because there were thousands of seagulls hovering around behind the ship feeding on the scraps of salmon that would float on the surface.

During breaks some of the crew took target practice with their slingshots at the birds that were flying around the ship. Of course some of the birds took target practice on the crew and the ship also, which had to be cleaned off each day.

The salmon would then be put into that new machine that was

supposed to improve and speed up the process of gutting and cleaning each salmon. Claims of "new and improved" turned into "it slices and dices," and wound up taking longer than expected sometimes in the first few shakedown runs after the machine would jam and choke on a few salmon. When it jammed, it sounded like a bone got caught in its throat and it couldn't wash it down.

Although most of the time the Ryan machine did do a pretty good job of cleaning fish when it didn't choke. When the salmon got about halfway through that machine and the entrails were scraped out of the fish, they would drop onto a small conveyor belt that took them to the grinder. As the guts made their way along the belt, a processing gal would intercept them, take the eggs and put them in a basket for the Japanese company technicians. The Japanese technicians who processed the eggs would put them into a large, circulating water tank that removed all of the blood. There were two of these tubs that were located between decks next to the blast freezers and were monitored constantly by the Japanese technicians.

The Japanese technicians would be there building small, wooden boxes for the eggs. With an air-compression staple gun, they would put together hundreds of boxes. When the eggs were clean, the technician would put a piece of waxed paper in the box as the liner. A layer of eggs would then be laid in the box with a powdered chemical sprinkled over them. Then more layers would be added until the box was full. The paper would be folded over and a top would be stapled on, sealing the whole mess for shipping.

Salmon eggs in Japan are a delicacy and at the current price per pound, we figured that a five-pound box of salmon eggs was worth about two hundred American dollars in Japan. No wonder it's a delicacy in Japan.

Most of the time during the first part of the salmon season at

False Pass, we were just getting used to the new and improved version of slow-downs and gut wars. If and when the salmon made it out the other end of the Ryan machine, the salmon would be grabbed up by one of the "slimers." Usually there were four or five people standing at the table with knife in hand waiting for the fish to come out of the Ryan machine so they could perform the final touch-up on each fish. Like I said before, the "new and improved" only worked some of the time. So it was up to the slimers at the end of the line to make sure the fish were clean and void of any blood and guts before the fish was graded and sorted.

Of course no day would be complete without the slime line gut wars.

This was a simple ordeal that usually took some imagination other than the all-out war of throwing salmon guts at each other, which sometimes occurred despite moral ethics. One female processor threatened to throw a handful of guts at a guy one day and was warned several times that she wouldn't be spared. Well she didn't believe him and let fly with a handful of guts at him, and the reprisal was fast and messy. He caught the guts and in one swift rebound motion chucked the guts right back at her, hitting her in the face. It was equality in the slime-line wars that kept everybody in check most of the time.

A person would always have to keep track of their gear so as not to fall victim to the gut wars. If a pair of gloves were left unattended, you could bet that when the owner returned and put their hand inside the glove, they'd be pulling it back out with salmon blood and guts on them. The ultimate accomplishment of the gut wars was to be able to successfully put some guts into someone's rubber boots without anybody knowing about it. Even though most people only had one pair of boots and would be in a world of hurt if they fell victim to the old "liver in the boot" routine, I knew of only one person that received that present. Rightfully so, it was a present that was well earned by this one person.

He was a new kid that had come on board at the end of the herring season who figured he could get away with pulling pranks on people as much as the Wookie and I could. The only problem was that his pranks were not very well appreciated by others. The Wookie and I had heard some negative comments about them and decided to make some of the crew a little happier. After all, the Wookie and I were the morale officers and we also agreed with each other that he was invading our territory of prank pulling.

The Wookie and I, after debating the question and effects of the outcome, decided that he should get a taste of some of his own medicine. We enlisted some help from the "ever eager to help" animal house guys for this small prank. Since our victim slept in one of the six-man units and not the animal house, it would be easier to get a few things of his without him knowing who it was. The Wookie and I figured that our little buddy needed to be cured of his urge to try and think that he was ready for the big leagues.

The season at False Pass was winding down with only a couple more days worth of fish to process. The Wookie and I felt the time was right at the next upcoming sleep break when all of the blast freezers were running full tilt. We had scoped out the whereabouts of all his belongings prior to him going to sleep.

At the end of a twenty-six hour work period and with all the blast freezers full, we finally got to hit the rack. However, the Wookie and I had to do some "fix it" work and needed the help of a couple of the animal house crew's help. About an hour after the rest of the crew was snoring away in dreamland, we set out on our mission. The Wookie and I went into the six-man unit and quietly took all of our victim's clothes and his seabag out of the bunkhouse. We left only his boots by the side of his bunk with a little present in them.

The Wookie dropped a couple of salmon livers in each boot just for the hell of it so he'd have that nice squishy feeling when he put his boots on.

We handed the seabag and the clothes to the two animal house guys who took them down to the blast freezers for us. When the Wookie and I arrived at the blast freezers we sent the animal house guys off to bed so we could finish our fix-it work. The Wookie and I soaked all his clothes with water and hung them in one of the blast freezers. It didn't take long for the blast freezers to do their job on his clothes. We went to sleep for about five hours ourselves, knowing that when it was time to get up and unload the blast freezers those clothes would be solid ice cubes.

When we woke up, we were just in time to hear the commotion going on in the bunkhouse.

As I left my stateroom on the upper deck, I made my way around the aft part of the main house where I was met with the sight of this guy wandering around in his underwear shouting and yelling that he wanted his clothes back. He demanded to know who took his clothes and where they were. He ran into the animal house and yelled at the guys in there, and he also went into the other six-man unit and yelled in there demanding his clothes back. He went over to the stairs to go down to the main deck but, getting halfway down them, came back up and tried one more time yelling for someone to give him his clothes back.

Just then the Wookie came up the stairs to the upper deck to go into the wheelhouse, but stopped and stared at this guy running around in his underwear yelling that he wanted his clothes back. The Wookie started laughing but managed to say he was just coming up here to try and find out whose clothes were hanging frozen in the blast freezer.

"Say what?" I asked with total astonishment in my voice.

"Yeah, somebody's clothes are frozen in one of the blast freezers," he said.

As our victim stood there in his underwear, he couldn't believe what he had just heard.

"How the hell am I going to go get my clothes looking like this?" he yelled.

Both the Wookie and I shrugged our shoulders and didn't reply. Then another crewman who was standing nearby made the suggestion that he could put on some rain gear to cover up with. So off he ran downstairs to the main deck where the rain gear was hung up close by. After putting on rain pants and a raincoat, he ran back up the stairs cursing about how cold he was and how the rain gear felt against his bare skin. He disappeared into his bunkhouse for a minute when all of a sudden the air turned blue again. I'm sorry, but I can't repeat all the swear words here or even remember how he put them together in a civil fashion, but the decibels inside that bunkhouse were loud enough to rattle the windows. The door burst open and out flew a pair of rubber boots along with a couple of salmon livers falling to the deck also. The Wookie and I couldn't maintain our composure and walked away laughing like a couple of hyenas.

I guess our victim somehow managed to get his clothes out of the blast freezer soon after that, because he was seen standing around in his rain gear in the laundry room with both dryers going full bore.

I sauntered into the processing house where the Wookie was getting the fluid fish pump ready for the last of the tenders to unload. I filled him in on all the details of our victim and his desperate attempt at drying his clothes out.

As the work got under way, one crew had already started emptying out the blast freezers between decks. The second part of the processing line consisted of slamming the baskets down on a big wooden block to break the salmon apart, dipping each basket of salmon in a special glaze tank, dumping the fish out on a large table, filling boxes with the frozen salmon, strapping the boxes closed and finally sending each box down a chute into the freezer hold.

Our ship held approximately one and a half million pounds of salmon when full. Usually there were three freezer rats (crewmen) that worked in the minus-fifteen-degree hold stacking boxes of salmon for hours on end. When it was meal time, they would climb out of the hold looking like snowmen. If any of them had mustaches or beards, they would have clumps of icicles hanging from them.

One time I joined the freezer rats for a lengthy period just to make sure all was going well in the bottom of the ship. I set up a conveyor line for the boxes of salmon so we didn't have to carry the sixty-pound boxes too far across the length of the hold. After six hours of huffing and puffing in sub-zero temperatures, I climbed out of the hold looking like a frozen walrus with long, white tusks hanging from my mustache and beard. When we climbed out of the hold, we felt like we were in the Bahamas and had to take off our insulated freezer suits. The outside temperature was only in the 40s but felt like the 80s.

As the entire crew worked on processing the last two tender loads of salmon, we knew the end of round one was near. Our processing manager and company man, Ron, wandered into the processing house and informed the Wookie and I that we were in the homestretch and as soon as we were done we could head for Bristol Bay. We also had a choice as to take a break and get some sleep or pound it out and keep working till we finished, then have a longer break before Bristol Bay.

The Wookie and I took a quick poll of some of the crew and it was decided by the vast majority to continue working until we were all done with False Pass salmon. At that time it looked like we could accomplish that task in a matter of hours. What figured to take ten or twelve hours somehow turned into another twenty-two hours, and that was on top of the twenty-six hours we were going on when we made the choice. Now I knew our brains were melting to have thought we could do that but, as it turned out, we wound up working forty-eight hours straight before we finished up at False Pass.

As the last salmon made its way through the slime line and was sent to the blast freezers, everybody in the processing house had saved some salmon guts and, as if a starting gun had gone off, everybody threw salmon guts at each other which signaled the end of round one.

The Wookie and I shut the line down and after a good eight hours worth of sleep, we were up early securing the booms and "picking the pick." As always, when we had new crewmen on board, the Wookie and I always chose the new guy to go down into the chain locker.

Chapter 11

THE FINAL FISH

As the sun rose over Mount Pavlof early in the morning, we made our final preparations as the ship got under way. The morning sky was lit up with the remaining colors of the sunrise as the days now began to get shorter. In the early morning chill, there was a clean, crisp feeling in the air as the ship once again headed west toward Unimak Pass. The sun shown a bright orange on the barren hills of tundra as our ship made way toward the Bering Sea. Having got a whole eight hours sleep the night before, the Wookie and I were in prime shape to continue with whatever prank tickled our fancy. After all, we had a few new prospects at our disposal that came aboard.

The voyage from False Pass on the Pacific Ocean side of the chain to our destination of the Ugashik River on the Bristol Bay side of the chain was only a three-day journey. As I was on the wheel, the Wookie took it upon himself to seek out someone to help him with a small detail. In the galley several crewmen were playing cards and watching movies. The Wookie asked one particular guy if he could help him for awhile down in engineering. The new crewman really couldn't refuse his request to help out and so off he went with the Wookie like a lamb to the slaughter. The Wookie told him that the return pressure valve to the seawater circulator pump was on the fritz and he and one of the engineers had to fix it. This entailed the Wookie and the engineer going into the fidley to fix the problem while the crewman stayed in the engine room with the main engine churning away, staring at a panel of gauges. The crewman was to tell them if any of the gauges changed while they worked on the valve.

Well first of all, when the Wookie walked into the wheelhouse, I could see that he had "that look" on his face that I had come to recognize over the past several months. As I finished taking a position fix on our course, I asked the Wookie what he was up to now.

"Oh, nothing really," he said. "I just have a guy sitting down in the engine room staring at that wall of old gauges," he added.

"Wait a minute you low-life," Captain Hook said looking up over the rim of his coffee cup. "Those gauges were bypassed last year when we put in the new water maker."

"Yeah, I know," said the Wookie. "I told him that the return pressure valve to the seawater circulator pump was broke and to let me know if any of those gauges changed while the engineer and I worked on the valve."

At this point I need to clarify this a little and tell you that there was no such thing as a return pressure valve to a seawater circulator pump onboard that ship. Captain Hook set his coffee cup down on the chart table and, looking at the Wookie with "that look" of his he always had when he knew the Wookie was up to something again said, "There is no such thing as a !*$#!*@! return pressure seawater whatever pump onboard this ship."

"I know that, but he doesn't know that," the Wookie retorted.

I just about fell out of my chair laughing at this comedy routine going on between the skipper and the Wookie.

"So he's sitting in the engine room watching a bunch of broken gauges while you're up here drinking coffee?" the skipper asked.

"Sure, why not?" said the Wookie.

"How long has he been there?" I asked.

"Oh, about an hour or so," the Wookie replied.

Captain Hook just shook his head, picked up his coffee cup and stared out the window knowing it would do no good to try and say anything more.

The Wookie and I left the wheelhouse and wandered down to the engine room where we found the crewman sitting on the workbench still watching that panel of gauges. The Wookie and I walked over to him and stood there staring at the non-functioning gauges also.

"Any of them change yet?" the Wookie hollered.

"Nope, nothing has changed here, still the same," the crewman hollered back.

"OK, we're almost done fixing that valve so we'll let you know when you can come up out of here," the Wookie told him.

And with that, the Wookie and I left him there and went up to the galley for a refill of coffee. Once in the galley, one of the animal house "animals" hollered across the room asking where "what's his name" was. The Wookie and I looked at each other and, not being able to contain ourselves, busted out laughing, spilling coffee on ourselves.

The Wookie proceeded to fill everyone in on this harmless little joke which brought raucous laughter from everyone in the galley.

After slurping down a few cups of mud and telling stories, we left the galley and went back down to engineering to get that crewman out of there.

"All right, we got her fixed now, you can stop watching those gauges now," he yelled.

"OK," the crewman said and headed up the ladder to the main deck.

After returning to the galley, one of the animal house guys asked him what he was doing in the engine room. He told him he was helping the engineer and the Wookie watch gauges while the engineer changed a valve in the fidley. Just then the engineer, Marvin, a crusty old sea dog, stepped through the door of the galley to grab a cup of coffee.

"Hey did you get that valve fixed yet?" the gauge-watching crewman hollered.

"What valve?" Marv asked. "What the hell are you talking about?"

"That return pressure valve to the seawater circulator. I was sitting in the engine room for over an hour watching those gauges on that panel down there," he griped.

Marv was a man of few words and really didn't have a clue as to what he was talking about.

"There's no such goddamned thing like that around here," he growled.

For just a second, all sound and time in the galley froze with the look on that poor crewman's face. They say a picture is worth a thousand words? Well the statement on his face when he heard those words was worth ten thousand words.

The entire galley erupted with laughter that probably could be heard all the way to Kodiak. That crewman, being embarrassed as he was, still managed to laugh along with the rest of the crew. He even joked about it too for a bit. I must say he was a good sport about the whole thing, which really helped break up the mundane traveling times.

The Wookie and I walked back up to the wheelhouse where we

told the skipper what had transpired down in the galley of how our victim found out that there was no such thing as a return pressure valve to a seawater circulator pump. Captain Hook laughed too, which was a relief on our part knowing that he wasn't mad about all the stuff we did. We figured he should have been used to us by now after several months of putting up with the two of us.

Once again traveling through Unimak Pass into Bristol Bay, we hugged the coastline heading east along the north side of the chain toward the Ugashik River. The other two processing ships that were running along off our port beam had already been deployed to the Egigik and Naknek rivers and had to travel several miles further up the chain.

As we neared the entrance to the Ugashik River, Captain Hook had to radio for a pilot boat to guide our ship up the river channel a short distance so as not to run aground in the shallow delta of the mouth. The mouth of the Ugashik River was very wide, almost a mile across, but was very shallow. Our ship drew nineteen feet of draft and was confined to the deeper water wherever we went in the many shallow fishing areas. We were led a short distance up the channel to a place just outside the town of Pilot Point where we could anchor for the remainder of the season.

The Wookie and I dropped the anchor as the skipper backed down on her to get a good hold in the mud. The season was set to open the following day and everything had to be ready to go again. That evening as I was splicing and repairing the extra mooring lines, the skipper came out of the wheelhouse and hollered down at me on the main deck to launch the lifeboat and head into Pilot Point. The owner was flying in to be on board for the remainder of the major part of the salmon season.

I stowed my splicing gear, grabbed my diddy bag and launched the lifeboat. By this time it was dark outside and navigating a river delta that I've never been on before proved to be somewhat of a challenge. As I left the ship, I could see the lights of Pilot Point on the distant shore. I made a beeline straight toward them hoping that even if I strayed out of the channel a little bit, I could still make it there.

The distance from the ship to the town was about one-quarter of a mile. Before traveling even half that distance, I all of a sudden came to a complete stop. Now I knew I was still surrounded by water, but when the waterline exceeds the depth of the water, you are most assuredly aground.

I sat there dumbfounded for a second as I quickly shut off the motor, wondering which way I had to go to find the channel. I stood up and looked around to see if I could find any indications or resemblance of deeper water. I didn't.

I stepped out of the boat into the water that was only a couple of feet deep. It was a strange feeling standing there in the dark completely surrounded by water for hundreds of yards in all directions. I grabbed the bowline and started walking toward shore dragging the sixteen-foot boat behind me. I was going to get to shore one way or another even if I had to drag the boat all the way there.

As I trudged along toward the lights of Pilot Point, the portable hand held radio that I had with me suddenly squawked to life with the sound of someone calling me. It was a guy on shore who was waiting there with our company owner for me to come pick up. I radioed back and told them that I was half way there but ran out of water deep enough to float the boat.

He asked me where I was in relation to him from our ship. Of course me being an experienced captain and knowing a thing or two about dead reckoning, I told him I was halfway there I reckon. Well unfortunately I didn't get the response I was hoping for.

Making light of the situation with the owner standing there who was probably very tired and not in a jovial mood didn't help me too much.

I had been walking in a zigzag pattern hoping to find the deeper water but my luck wasn't too good. I pulled out the flashlight I had with me and shined it toward town.

"OK, I see you now," he said over the radio. "You need to go more to your left to get into the channel."

I took a left turn and, walking about fifty feet, found deeper water. I was able to navigate the rest of the way into shore where the owner and one of the local fishermen who piloted boats in and out of Pilot Point greeted me. After a quick crash course on dead reckoning back out to the ship, the owner and I made it there without having me imitate a sled dog pulling the boat.

The next morning arrived way too fast for my liking. The nightmare started playing out again in real life as the season opened with a vengeance. The dozens of fishing boats came to us two and three times per day with their boats full of salmon. It was a steady routine of filling the blast freezers, getting three or four hours of sleep, then emptying them again. We would fill them as fast as we could empty them.

Day after day the entire crew would be up to their ears in salmon. Even the skipper and the first mate worked right along with the rest of us during this time. They worked with us as the steady stream of salmon and long hours assaulted us.

After two weeks of almost non-stop work, the crew was starting to feel the effects. During breaks, most of the processing crew would find a pallet of cardboard or fifty-pound bags of rock salt and go to sleep on them. It was pretty hard to get yourself moving again after stopping even for fifteen minutes due to sheer exhaustion.

The gut wars seemed to diminish with most people being to

tired and not having enough energy even to pick up a salmon heart and throw it at the foreman.

Along about the third week an unexpected break from our misery came from the fish and game department. The river net fishery had been closed until further notice. The escapement goal of fish going up the river had to be met and closing the river to fishing was the standard practice. This break in the action allowed us to catch up and even finish the amount of salmon we had yet to process.

When we finished the last batch out of the blast freezers, I remember staggering to my bunk and falling into it fully clothed. When I woke up, I found that I had slept for thirteen hours straight. I stumbled out onto the upper deck still half-asleep just in time to catch the sight of one of the "animals" running around the corner away from the skipper's head. As I entered the head, I froze in the doorway to survey the damage done. The interior decorating left much to be desired. Someone had TP'd the whole place. I thought at first that this was just an inconvenience and that there was no real harm done. But as I was cleaning up the toilet paper I figured I didn't need to get mad and I didn't need to get even, I was going to get ahead.

I didn't care who did the deed, I was going to go for the flock shot and see how many I could get with one shot. I didn't say anything to anyone about the little mess in the head as I went about my business as though nothing ever happened.

The temporary closure only lasted a couple of days during the peak of the run, then it was back to work. That was a well-deserved break for us because as it turned out for all concerned, the salmon run in the Ugashik River that year was the biggest ever recorded. In fact one of the other processing ships that was sent to the Naknek River, which usually has the biggest run of salmon, was pulled out of there due to an average return and brought back to our location to help with the tremendous amount of fish that were there.

Our hold was getting very full as we continued processing day and night. A Japanese tramp ship arrived as we were about ready to bust at the seams because we had no more room. We shortened our two processing lines to make up a third line so we could offload the fish even as we kept on processing them. Here we were, swamped with working two lines and offloading the boxes of frozen salmon while tied to a tramp ship, when the weather decided that we could use some more excitement.

The water got rougher as the wind blew harder. Our ship and the tramp ship were being bounced around like fishing bobbers with hungry fish biting at the bait below them. The Wookie and I broke out the extra mooring lines and ran three more of them to the tramper to keep the two ships snugged up tight. As the cargo nets full of boxes of salmon were lifted out of our hold, swung across to the tramp ship and lowered into their hold, it got more and more dangerous as it was almost impossible to raise and lower the swinging cargo nets. The skipper called a halt to the madness of trying to offload for the time being till the storm passed.

After about three hours of sleep I was dragged out of my nice warm bunk by the first mate. After sleepwalking to the galley to get an IV of coffee for myself, I went up the stairs to the wheelhouse. As I made it to the upper deck, I took about four steps toward the wheelhouse door and ran into an invisible wall of ammonia that knocked me backwards and right on my butt. I couldn't see, I couldn't breathe and had to feel along the deck for the stairs to crawl down them to escape it.

A line that ran along the back of the processing house had given way and was leaking the highly concentrated substance that was used as the freezing agent in the system. The engineers found out about the leak at the same time I did and had to shut the system down till they could replace the line. With the blast freezers full of salmon and shut down for the time being, we went back to work concentrating on offloading more of the cargo hold since the storm had quieted down some.

While the crew was working in the hold, I took the opportunity to leave a few presents in the animal house. I strategically placed them so as not to be easily found by the occupants for some time. I figured a few days is all it would take for the aroma to get unbearable even for those guys.

A few hours later we were back up and running full bore again finishing off the last of the salmon. As the blast freezers were being emptied, the cargo nets continued to fly around as we were still bouncing up and down in a swell. We were on the countdown to the last box of salmon. Our freezer foreman, Nick, while running the pallet jack bringing the pallets of salmon out of the blast freezers, announced that we were on the last freezer load. The change in the crew that occurred was unbelievable. The reality of knowing that the end was near was like a shot in the arm for the entire crew.

Forget about milking the clock, forget about the gut wars and forget about sleep, this crew was on a mission now. Everybody just wanted to get done since it had been a grueling month there where the body was pushed to the limit and beyond.

When the final fish made it's way into the last box and that box was put aboard the Japanese tramp ship, we all applauded one another for a job well done. As the machinery was shut down and the large deck hatches put back in place, there was silence as we all stood looking at one another hardly believing that this time had finally arrived.

After a quick break, the crew set about cleaning up and getting ready to depart Bristol Bay. I was sitting in the galley listening to some of the processing crew talk about how much work they did and the hours they put in for that last week and I knew they weren't kidding. I was curious myself as to the amount of hours I had put in and decided to go get my time card. After adding up the hours worked, I realized why I was so dead tired and miserable. In seven days I had worked one hundred and forty hours. That's not bad considering that there is only one hundred and sixty-eight total hours in an entire week.

As the cleanup progressed, the Wookie and I made ready to haul in the mooring lines because we were headed back to Old Harbor on Kodiak Island.

The owner had been on board during the whole time the ship was in the Ugashik River and, before leaving the ship, he told the skipper that we all had done a great job. In fact we were to receive a small percentage of the profits because of the high volume of fish we processed.

The total weight of salmon from our ship was just shy of two million pounds that we processed and delivered to the Japanese. After we said our good-byes to the tramp ship and were leaving the area, I was sure the Japanese wouldn't miss the four salmon I donated to the animal house.

Chapter *12*

BOMBS AWAY

Captain Hook and I took the first six-hour watch that morning as we were getting under way. I sat down at the chart table to plot our course while the skipper set the speed and yelled down the hawspipe to the engineers. This would be our fourth time through Unimak Pass this year and luckily each time previously the weather had been good, which is usually a rare thing for this part of Alaska. We had another eight days of sailing time ahead of us. The salmon processing lines had to be dismantled with all the gear either stowed or ready to be taken off the ship as soon as we got to Old Harbor. Just like in the beginning and for most of the time, the ship would be processing crab again.

Even though the salmon season for us was over with, we still had a lot of work to do. The engineers during this time were the busiest. They kept the ship together and running like a well-oiled machine. They mainly built the processing lines with some help from the rest of us. Welding, cutting and pre-fabrication work was done by the engineers so that the processors could work smarter and not harder. To say they were great would be an understatement. They were better than great, and the rest of the crew knew it too.

While the ship headed for Unimak Pass, most of the processing crew took turns working each day. The average workday while under way was anywhere from twelve to sixteen hours long. Some of the crew would keep working while others would either sleep or play cards in the galley. For most of the crew, the time spent working on tearing down the salmon line was a piece of cake compared to the actual processing. The ship's main crew, the skipper, first mate and the two deckhands worked the usual six hours on and six hours off navigating the ship.

Some of the crew wanted to break out the beer while enroute back to Old Harbor. They figured they could get drunk while the ship was under way since they didn't have to work.

"Hey, this could be a real party to celebrate the end of the salmon season for us," one of the animals said.

"And the girls can dance for us too like they did at False Pass and we could have a real floating bar here," added another one of the animal house guys.

I sat there in the galley listening to this bullshit and, after hearing these guys whine and complain, I decided to fill them in on how I made a floating bar one time.

One year I was skippering a one hundred and twenty foot buying barge on the Kenai River during the salmon season. I had a crew of eight that worked with me unloading the gillnet boats that would come in to offload their catch each night. The boats would leave early in the morning and head out into Cook Inlet to set their nets out. They could only fish from 0700 to 1900 each day. While all the fishing boats were out catching salmon, I had to have all the gear ready to offload sixty small boats and three tenders.

My barge was firmly anchored from both ends in the river channel with a floating dock tied to it that was attached to the shore. I was located only three-quarters of a mile from the mouth of the river.

Usually during the day there wasn't much to do while waiting for the boats to come back in to offload. In my spare time after my morning work was done, I would fish off the side of my barge catching salmon as they passed by right under me. I caught salmon one after another, with several of them being huge Chinook salmon weighing anywhere from forty to eighty pounds.

One fine day when the weather was just perfect, my first mate Dave and myself got a hair-brained idea to have some fun other than fishing. We had noticed that in the Kenai area there were enormous tides. Some of the time there were twenty-five-foot tides, which really put one hell of a lot of back pressure on our Transvac fluid fish pump when pumping fish two hundred feet up the dock to the sorting pad during a low tide.

During the day after low tide was over and the flood tide started in, the flow of the river would slow its downstream journey to a standstill, then start flowing back upstream. The lower river area would flood with water until the incoming tide was at its end.

As the water flowed back upstream, salmon, seals, and even beluga whales would venture up the Kenai for a mile or so swimming around in the gray, glacier silt water.

Dave and I had all our work done and had several hours of free time on our hands. As we stood on the deck watching this daily occurrence, I got the bright idea of floating up river with all the fish. Dave said it sounded great but we needed to take our beer along with us. We had a bad habit of drinking a lot of beer during our down time since we were not a seagoing vessel. We were attached to shore, which meant we were almost a bunch of landlubbers.

I always kept four totes of ice on board to keep the many cases of beer we had ice-cold at all times. Dave thought we should get ourselves a cooler full of ice and beer to take with us in the boat.

"Boat? What boat?" I asked.

"Our seine skiff that's tied to the dock," he said.

I told him that we were not taking the skiff because I had another idea of floating upriver.

"The survival suits that we have stowed in the line locker," I exclaimed. "We can put them on and float up river with the tide since they are dry suits."

I told him that we needed something to put the beer on so as not to dump them in the river. As I was standing there looking at the storage yard of the fish plant next door to our sorting pad, I spied a large innertube leaning against the fence. A little, dim light came on in the void between my ears and I told Dave that I had the perfect idea for a floating bar. I wandered over to the storage yard and performed a quick snatch-and-roll of the soon-to-be-floating bar. I walked back to my side of the fence and proceeded to build a beautiful platform using a piece of plywood strapped to that large innertube.

We donned our survival suits and placed a large cooler full of ice and beer on this floating platform. We tied a line from the floating bar to each of us so as not to get separated from our beer. We lowered ourselves into the water from off our dock and slowly paddled out into the flood current.

I must say even I was surprised at how well we stayed afloat slowly drifting upstream with beer cans in hand enjoying the scenery. As we floated up river, every now and then a salmon would jump out of the water very close to us and a few times they would run into us not being able to see in the gray, glacial silt. As we passed by a few of the upriver fish plants, several people would stop and stare at us. We waved at everyone we saw as we floated along in the mid-day sunshine, paddling over to a couple of the fish plants to answer questions from the more curious spectators.

Dave and I floated upriver for almost two miles before we came to a halt. As if the incoming current lost all of its strength, the river reversed itself and began to push us back downriver. This of course is what we expected but we were a little surprised at the speed at which we were traveling back toward our starting point. The drift trip down river took about half the time and we had to swim a lot harder to line ourselves up with our dock, otherwise we would have been swept out into Cook Inlet. We arrived back at our barge, unloaded the floating bar, and got out of those survival suits. We stowed the bar and the beer, turned up the Jimmy Buffett music as loud as the boom box would go, then sat there and waited for the boats to come in. Unfortunately, we never got the chance to float again that summer.

By the time I got through with the story, I had to get back up to the wheelhouse or the skipper would have hung me from the king post. I left the card players to their own tales and stories and walked up the port-side stairs to the upper deck so as to pass by the bunk houses and the animal house. On my way to the wheelhouse, I poked my head inside the animal house. We were three days into our journey back to Old Harbor and I wondered if anybody had noticed anything different yet. At this particular time there was no one in the animal house and it was apparent that the inhabitants of this abode either all smelled the same as rotting fish or their sinuses didn't work at all. I quickly pulled my head back out of the doorway and headed to the wheelhouse.

I sat down at the chart table to take a position fix while the skipper continued working on paperwork. As the miles slowly slid by under our keel and the boredom of being under way seemed like we were never going to get back to Kodiak Island, we made the most of it the best we could.

Late the next day when I was in the galley having dinner, one of the animals from the animal house came into the galley and stated to some of the other guys in there that something reeked real bad in their bunk house. When asked what it was, he said he didn't know but it smelled like rotten fish and had smelled like that for two days now. One of the other animals piped up and echoed the same thing.

"Yeah, it really stinks in there, like someone died or something," he said.

I left the galley without saying a word and ventured up to the upper deck by way of the animal house again to see if anyone was around. Still not seeing anyone there, I headed for my bunk to get some sleep before my next watch.

Next morning at 0600 when the skipper and I relieved the first mate and the Wookie, I went to the galley to fill our thermos with coffee to have in the wheelhouse with us. After I filled the thermos with that tasty, black mud and was headed back up to the wheel-house, I heard yelling coming from the aft deck. I walked around the main house and was met by the site of several guys milling around out on the deck outside the animal house. They were chok-ing, gagging and complaining about the stench inside their bunkhouse.

A couple of them started searching around the bunkhouse and to their dismay found a couple of rotting salmon buried under some Playboy magazines under one of the bunks. They came out the open door carrying that stinky stuff and proceeded to throw the whole mess overboard.

"Who the hell did that?" one guy yelled.

"Well we'd better check out the rest of the place to make sure there's no more of that crap in there," another guy said.

As the search continued for more rotten salmon, this little endeavor turned into a complete cleansing of the animal house, which was long overdue. They found the other two salmon rolled up in another pile of papers and magazines in one corner of the room and deposited them over the side of the ship. Someone got the cleaning gear and the animal house received a good cleaning.

I walked back to the wheelhouse and informed the skipper that a complete cleaning of the animal house was under way with all of the animals participating.

"What the hell did you do to them?" he asked me.

"Well, let's just say the smell must have finally gotten to them and they're cleaning the place up," I said.

"Ace! What the hell did you do to them?" he barked again.

"They decided to clean the whole place on their own," I answered.

"Bullshit! You know all I have to do is ask one of them and they'll tell me," he said.

So I proceeded to tell him the whole story of the joke they played with the toilet papering of the head and how I decided to get my revenge on the whole group. He sat there taking it all in, then just shook his head. For the rest of the voyage back to Old Harbor, things went smoothly with no earth-shattering events taking place on board, except for the day we were arriving at Old Harbor.

The Wookie and I made fast the mooring lines as the ship came to rest at the dock we had left several months before. It was a welcomed sight to be back here but unfortunately not a restful one. We now had to unload all the salmon gear off the ship, take it to the warehouse and bring all the crab gear back to the ship. Setting up the crab processing line would only take a few days to complete and then we could call it a season.

The main office set up the flight reservations for the Captain, first mate, the Wookie and myself to fly out of there back to Seattle four days later. I already had my seabags packed and ready to go when we hit the dock.

The next night while the four of us were having dinner in the galley, Captain Hook let the cat out of the bag and told the Wookie about the case of scotch that he had gotten from the captain of the tramp ship. That was the first time all season the Wookie was speechless. The first mate then came up with a plan for a good-bye to the ship and the rest of the crew that was staying on board for the start of the crab season.

Late that night the Wookie and I went into the galley and proceeded to fill plastic bags with flour. We filled and tied them shut to have them ready for our departure. The next day while I was rummaging around in the forward food storage locker between decks, I came across a box of herring and a small gallon bucket of salmon eggs. I felt this would be a perfect addition for our good bye.

With the work completed by the next day and the crab line ready to go, the four of us met in the wheelhouse for the last time. Captain Hook broke out that case of scotch he'd gotten from the skipper of that Japanese tramp ship. The Wookie stood there in total disbelief as the skipper told him the story of how he pulled that little stunt on him by being in the hold of their ship when that female came over in the cargo net.

Captain Hook poured the Wookie, the first mate and himself each a glass of scotch. then handed me a beer since I didn't drink scotch. After a short speech from the skipper telling us how great it was to have us as his crew, we drank a toast to the end of the season.

Early the next morning with our heads throbbing from the many toasts we made for several hours and the stories we re-hashed from the past six months, we were able to get our gear to that little dirt path they called a runway. Before we left the ship, the skipper asked Ron, the processing manager, to have everybody he could out on the decks as we flew over the ship to wave good-bye.

After waiting fifteen minutes there in the early-morning coolness, our plane arrived. We loaded our bags in the aft compartment except for two grocery bags. These bags accompanied us inside the plane. Captain Hook gave the pilot fifty dollars to make several low, slow passes over the ship. At first the pilot was a little hesitant but agreed to help us with our plan.

With five of us in a six-seater, the plane lifted up off the runway and climbed to an altitude safe enough for him to make a sharp turn. The plane with its sliding windows was the perfect thing. We came in low and straight on the ship's bow for the first pass over her.

"Bomb's away!" we all yelled and proceeded to drop eight bags of flour, herring and salmon eggs on the ship.

"Direct hit on her main deck and house," I said.

We saw the crew that was out on the deck scramble for cover. Our pilot made another sharp bank to the right then back to the left again as we made another run right up her stern.

"Bombs away again!" the Wookie yelled as eight more bags exploded along the length of the ship. Captain Hook asked how many bombs we had left and I said we had four more. The pilot made another turn and came in again dead center on her bow. We let go dropping the last four bags of flour, hitting the top of the processing house and the wheelhouse. As the plane made its turn out over the water and we headed for Kodiak, the pilot dipped the wings several times as we said our final good-bye to that ship and crew for the year.

The flight home was a quiet, sullen time to think and reflect back on the past six months that consumed our entire existence. After arriving in Seattle five hours later, I still had to board another plane and fly out to Port Angeles. With the excitement and anticipation of arriving home soon, I thought to myself that this had been one of the most interesting adventures I had ever accomplished in a long time.

Catching a taxi at the Port Angeles airport, I arrived at my home looking like a ruffed up, hairy bear that just came out of hibernation. I had the taxi driver go to the front door with a bouquet of flowers to hand to my wife while I walked into the house via the back door. I almost scared the hell out of her when she turned around with the flowers in hand and saw me standing there.

She really didn't care for the hairy face and long hair down to my back but made an exception at that time. I did put my seabags down first though before settling in and tending to my wife. Getting used to being back at home and realizing that I didn't have to work twenty-four hours in a row that night, I continued to reflect back on the previous six months. After several hours back in my own comfortable home, I arrived at a final conclusion.

After experiencing very long hours of work and being away from my family, I swore an oath to myself that I was never going to do that again for as long as I lived.

Author's Biographical Note

Gary Gorss was born and raised in Los Angeles where he first started fishing out of Santa Monica at age twelve. In 1970 he moved to Neah Bay, Washington where he lived with his aunt and uncle. All through high school he continued to work as a deckhand on charter and commercial boats. At the age of fourteen Gary bought and fished a small commercial troller and fished off the coast of Washington for several years.

He has been a licensed captain since 1980 having worked and fished in Washington and Alaska. At present, he and his wife Serena, live in Port Angeles, Washington where he still captains a charter boat each year out of Neah Bay for halibut.

ISBN 1553950061-5